FIDEL &
MALCOLM
X

FIDEL&
MALCOLM X

Memories of a Meeting

Rosemari Mealy

Black Classic Press
Baltimore

FIDEL & MALCOLM X
Memories of a Meeting

Library of Congress Control Number: 2013904225

ISBN: 9781574780581

Printed in the United States by BCP Digital Printing,
an affiliate company of Black Classic Press, Inc.

Cover design by Anthony Lisby.

To review or purchase Black Classic Press books, visit
www.blackclassicbooks.com.

You may also obtain a list of titles by writing to:
Black Classic Press
c/o List
P.O. Box 13414
Baltimore, MD 21203

Publisher's Note to the Black Classic Press edition

More than five decades have lapsed since September 1960, when African American Muslim leader Malcolm X welcomed Cuban President Fidel Castro to a midnight meeting at Harlem's Black-owned Hotel Theresa. Castro and his delegation had come to New York to attend the UN General Assembly, but the management of the Manhattan hotel they had booked refused to house them. Upon learning of their plight, Malcolm invited the Cuban emissaries to "come uptown" to Harlem, where he claimed they would be greeted "with open arms."

Indeed, Harlemites by the thousands gave Castro a rousing, even magnificent welcome, keeping a round-the-clock vigil—in the pouring rain—outside his balcony window. To Harlem's masses, unfazed by the red baiting and anti-Cuba hysteria of the day, Castro was that "bearded revolutionary" who had "told White America to go to hell." They crowded the streets to see and cheer the Cuban delegation and its then thirty-four-year-old revolutionary leader.

Sadly, however, little is said, even today, about the far-reaching conversations that took place between Malcolm and Fidel that September evening. Only three newsmen were allowed to join them: two representatives and a photographer from "the Negro press." They noted that the two leaders exchanged pleasantries, then spoke candidly, through their interpreters, about self-determination and national liberation. Though language differences proved a formidable barrier, author Rosemari Mealy maintains that "the respect that both men expressed towards each other...solidified the ties of friendship between the Cuban revolution and the relentless struggles of the African American people."

In this slim yet significant volume, Mealy, along with contributors Elombe Brath, LeRoi Jones (Amiri Baraka), Sarah E. Wright, and Bill Epton, compile the recollections of a number of persons who played important roles in this historic summit. They add to these their own perspectives—as historians, poets, journalists, and political activists—on the two leaders and the revolutionary movements they spawned. The combined reflections, coupled with Malcolm's and Fidel's own writings about the encounter and rare photographs of the two men together, yield an authentic accounting of a remarkable meeting of the minds.

Contents

Acknowledgements 1

Introduction 2

Chronology 10

Cuba, Fidel, Harlem and Us 14

From the Shelburne to the Theresa 32

Going upstairs: Malcolm X greets Fidel 41

Cuba Libre *by LeRoi Jones (Amiri Baraka)* 62

Cuba: A declaration of conscience by Afro Americans 79

Declaration of the African American delegation 81

Notes on contributors 85

Index 87

For Assata, Sam and Marc

Acknowledgements

To John T. Patterson, Jr., publisher of the *New York Citizen-Call*, for his invaluable support and for putting at my immediate disposal rare issues of the paper. To Georgina Chabau, Marguerita Delgado, Fernando García and the Americas department of the Central Committee of the Communist Party of Cuba for being there as both friends and colleagues. To Preston Wilcox for introducing me to the authentic sources and generously sharing his invaluable archives. To Esperanza Martel. Brother Hakim Shabazz of Tampa, Florida and 125th Street. To Dave Silver for directing me to the Fair Play for Cuba committee documents. To Amiri Baraka for being politically consistent and his opportune article *Cuba Libre*. To Marguerita Samad-Matias. To Mary Murray for her editing skills and wisdom that chided me to "just do it." To Gil Noble of ABC's "Like it is." To Don Rojas and the staff at the *Amsterdam News*; the Schomburg Center for Research in Black Culture; the UN Library; and the Tamiment Institute Library at New York University. To Michelle Hayes — my new friend! To Linda Prout for keeping the tapes rolling. To Muhammad Ahmad, Bill Sales, William Strickland and Abdul Aklamit. To Clarence Davis. To my research assistant Watson St. John Batiste. To David Deutschmann of Ocean Press, who gave priority to this project. To my colleagues Sally O'Brien, Zinzele Khosan and Consuelo Corrietjir of WBAI's *Cuba in Focus*: herewith is my contribution to "another viewpoint." To Prensa Latina and *Bohemia* for their photos. To Aissa García. Finally, to my Sister Lillian and all of my friends and associates who carried on for me so that I could meet my deadlines.

Special thanks to: Fidel Castro Ruz, Casa de las Américas and the Center for the Study of the Americas, Casa de Africa, the Cuban Institute for Friendship with the People (ICAP), the Center for the Study of Ethnology and Anthropology, and to the numerous historians, artists, internationalists and translators all of whom worked to make the *Malcolm X in the 90's Symposium* a success.

1

Introduction

More than one hundred invitations were mailed to various members of the African American community in the United States. The list included academics and scholars, activists and lawyers, publishers and journalists, and others who have positioned themselves as "experts" on the life and times of Malcolm X (El-Hajj Malik El-Shabazz). The names of several family members and friends had also been handed to me as possible participants in the now historic Havana gathering known as the *Malcolm X Speaks in the 90's Symposium*, held in the Cuban capital, May 22-24, 1990.

Each invitation was followed up with a telephone call(s) and personal visits to offices and homes, catching some on the move in clubs, restaurants, airports, and even gymnasiums. At social gatherings, I talked up the conference. Many of those invited had personally known Malcolm X. Every effort was spent in conveying the importance of attending the symposium while, in telephone call after call, I reminded my listener that one's mere presence as an observer would symbolically acknowledge the importance of the task, given that Cuba's Casa de las Americas had undertaken to host the seminar. A number of scholars were also invited to present papers and take part in the panel discussion with their Cuban counterparts.

Sadly, far too many of the responses to the invitations ranged from hostility to ambivalence, while the majority never responded at all. On more than one occasion, I was dismayed at the reluctance and skepticism of those lacking the ability to understand the significance of the forum.

A number of the highly-paid scholars sought a "free ticket and hotel accommodation," bolstered by requests for four figure honoraria. Upon hearing that neither was forthcoming — as it had been for some in the past, before hard times had hit the revolution — they quickly learned of crowded calendars or suddenly remembered prior commitments. Meanwhile, in the same quivering voice, the invitation was declined.

I suspect that in most instances the virulent and negative reactions were driven by anti-communist sentiments. How dare Cuba "claim Malcolm X," I was told by one irate scholar, whose own arrogance was only surpassed by the curt young rap artist who insisted that she would need to "check out the organizers" of the conference before accepting the invitation. In that particular case, the host had even agreed to fund the young lady's entire round-trip airfare from their meager resources. We had agreed that a major involvement would come from the youth whom we termed the voices of the new generation of African Americans reclaiming Malcolm as a part of their own struggle.

Fortunately, there were those worthy young warriors who came forward and accepted the challenge. They had the wisdom, scope and vision to capture the importance of the conference. These youthful activists paid their own way to Havana, etching their contributions into the history which is continuously being made by a new generation of African Americans.

The day our plane left for Havana with a spirited and excited delegation I immediately left the trials behind in Miami. We were welcomed to Cuba at the airport by officials of the Communist Party's department of the Americas, poet Nancy Morejón of Casa, representatives from the Center for the Studies of the Americas and our own "Sista" leader in exile, Assata Shakur. The composition of the U.S. delegation represented some of the best of the youth-activist-scholars community, African American women and men whose daily lives symbolized all that Malcolm represented.

The three-day conference was held under the auspices of two of Cuba's most prestigious institutions: Casa de las Américas (Casa) and the Center for the Study of the Americas (CEA). Meeting in Casa's spacious auditorium, in attendance were hundreds of visitors, observers and international guests from the Caribbean and Africa, including Ghana's Ambassador to Cuba, His Excellency Kofi Nyidevu Awoonor. Also joining the African American delegation from Conakry Guinea was Kwame Toure (Stokley Carmichael). The Cuban scholars brought an added dimension to the three days of intense dialogue, debate and exchange which focused on one of the African American people's more important leaders.

The life of Malcolm X, the historic figure who was maligned in the country of his birth by the most despotic of rulers and venous of critics, was accorded respect here in Cuba.

4   Fidel and Malcolm X

Cubans were fortunate to have access to the works of Malcolm X years ago: their publishing houses were some of the first to translate his ideas into a foreign language. In Cuban language schools, Malcolm's speeches are required texts for future translators and interpreters.

For Havana to host the symposium was clearly a recognition of Malcolm's contribution to the worldwide struggle for justice and equality. In the view of many, it was an important contribution to the internationalizing of Malcolm X thought.

As the symposium ended, the delegation spent several days roaming the island, visiting historical sites in the old city and modern housing developments, family health centers, schools and cultural institutions. There was a precious visit to the famous Isle of Youth, in pre-revolutionary days known as the "Isle Of Pines", where its infamous prison and torture dungeon entombed political dissidents and political prisoners.

One early morning, laden with cameras, tape recorders and bountiful energy, the group boarded a transport plane for the flight to the Isle of Youth. There they visited the prison where the revolutionaries of Moncada and the July 26 Movement crafted the last stages of the struggle against the dictatorship of Fulgencio Batista — a dictatorship backed by Washington.

The eerie silence of the place envelops you as you explore this cavern of horror whose blueprints were sketched by the hands of U.S. architects. It is now preserved as a reminder to the sacrifices made in the call to freedom that culminated in the triumph of the Cuban revolution and the end to what was once Washington's most cherished colony.

Later our emotions ran even higher when we were greeted by hundreds of African youth attending school on scholarship in this plush green terrain. These are the children of South Africa, Namibia, Angola and Mozambique — many having survived apartheid massacres in the refugee camps of southern Angola, or orphaned by U.S.-funded terrorist groups such as Jonas Savimbi's National Union for the Total Independence of Angola (UNITA) and the Mozambique National Resistance (MNR or RENAMO) bandits. The noble mandate of Cuba's internationalism had reached out to nourish these children in her bosom when the rest of the world had turned callous heads.

Spontaneously, the youth extended their friendship to

Malcolm's disciples. After an elaborate cultural presentation of songs, poetry and indigenous dances presented with skill, beauty and feeling, we were escorted through the open and spacious school grounds. The children proudly gave us a tour of their libraries, classrooms and laboratories. These "survivors" confidently proclaimed to their visiting cousins the real dictates of freedom from the standpoint of Africa's future. Afterwards, we walked through the gardens and citrus groves where the students cultivate and harvest their own food. Here, there are no lines drawn between the world of scholarly pursuits and "learning by doing" in order to teach self-sufficiency. Clear about their mission, the students emphasized how their knowledge would be returned to Africa after studies were completed.

The Isle of Youth visit took place on the heels of Nelson Mandela's release from prison and the Namibian independence celebrations. Our mood was electrified by the time we said our goodbyes; an indelible mark was in the hearts of we, who are so displaced throughout the diaspora. Perhaps some of us felt a little like Malcolm when he too had left the continent of Africa for the last time:

> In the plane, bound for Monrovia, Liberia to spend a day, I knew that after what I had experienced in the Holy Land, the second most indelible memory I would carry back to America would be the Africa seething with serious awareness of itself, and of Africa's wealth, and of her power, and of her destined role in the world.

Cuba had been a sort of "Holy Land" for us while one could not escape the fact that these children, trained under socialism on this island just 90 miles from the shores of the United States, would some day play their role in Africa's destiny.

Our final night in Cuba was spent as guests of President Fidel Castro.

How did the idea of the symposium come into being? It occurred during one of the many marathon conversations which always seem to break at dawn between myself and exiled freedom-fighter Assata Shakur. We compare the ideological influences of Malcolm upon our own political development to the influence he has had on revolutionary thought throughout the world. Assata and I often share notes on the rising phenomena and the rethinking of Malcolm's thought among today's African American youth. One night together we began to plant the seed of an idea that blossomed into the international symposium — a strategy we saw as consistent with our personal and collective commitment to carry forth Malcolm's teachings.

In a short period of time, we drafted an outline and circulated it among our mutual Cuban associates who shared our ideals. Several scholars had even hinted at the possibility of organizing some form of commemoration of Malcolm on the 65th anniversary of his birth.

On leaving the island, I felt very optimistic. Assata's task was to circulate our proposal to friends at Casa de las Américas.

In August 1989, I learned that Casa de las Américas agreed to host the symposium. I was being asked to take on the responsibility of contacting the many Malcolm scholars in the United States to assist in proposing themes and panel ideas for this encounter. I was also asked to secure and immediately send several copies of rare books and other sources so that the Cuban scholars could begin the arduous task of preparing papers. The more than 30-year U.S. blockade undermines and encumbers Cuban scholars in pursuit of projects involving the use of research materials on subjects relating to issues in the United States.

In addition, I was to make the travel arrangements and pick up any and all loose ends. I did not hesitate in accepting these responsibilities because Assata and I had felt that once the word was out people would jump at this opportunity to travel to Cuba for the symposium. How wrong we both were.

I first set out to form a broad organizing committee. It soon became clear that the project may have been a priority for me, but the support and commitments from academics and intellectuals would be minimal.

My best bet was to sink the proposal ideas deep into the community of activists to which I was intimately linked both as an organizer, educator and journalist. From this group I elicited support. What now remained was firming up schedules and individual commitments which would ensure the participation of the scholars from the United States.

The scholars who lent their greatest support were invariably connected to the activist community. A national pilgrimage to

Malcolm's hometown of Omaha, Nebraska, had also been planned for the same time as the Cuba symposium. This unfortunate conflict necessitated the absence of several major figures who had been invited to Cuba. We were literally working in a four to five month time frame. Two weeks before the symposium, I was informed by the Havana organizing committee that a book display and photo exhibit was being prepared and I had to immediately send down books and photos of Malcolm as well as scenes of Harlem and other memorabilia from the period.

I was given the name of a photographer, known for his extensive collection of Malcolm photographs. After several days of frantically trying to contact someone who knew him, I finally unearthed a phone number. Unfortunately, the photographer would not budge on lending even one photo for the exhibit (even with a promise of full credits) nor was he able to attend the conference. Near the final hour, as fate would maneuver, Clarence Davis, an eminent and veteran photographer from the *New York Daily News* came to my rescue. He immediately put me in touch with a valuable source for rare photos of Malcolm that arrived in Havana just in time to grace the walls of the Casa de las Américas library at the official opening ceremony of the symposium.

I worked out of my home, without a funding source, proper office space, access to fax machines, monies for mailing and telephone calls or for that matter, none of the other little amenities one takes for granted in organizing a major conference, much less one of the international magnitude we had embarked upon. As usual, my family and friends, some of whom I have acknowledged, provided support during moments when I truly doubted whether we could hold up our end of the planning.

The timing of the symposium also commemorated the 30th anniversary of the historic 1960 meeting between Malcolm X and Fidel Castro at Harlem's Hotel Theresa. The respect that both men expressed towards each other during that brief encounter solidified the ties of friendship between the Cuban revolution and the relentless struggles of the African American people.

For the first time, the authentic voices of those compatriots who had played some role in the brief but historic encounter between Fidel and Malcolm X would be documented. In this way, the 1990 symposium was directly responsible for the conception of this book.

It was an unforgettable moment one afternoon when Cuba's former UN ambasador, Raúl Roa Kouri, and renowned Cuban journalist Reinaldo Peñalver addressed the symposium, mesmerizing the participants with their vivid and colorful stories, reflections and memories — much of it untold — of the famed encounter between two of the greatest leaders of the 20th century.

It was Raúl Roa, we learned, who really should be credited for arranging — from the Cuban side — the logistics of that meeting. A phone call by Roa to a mutual acquaintance of both he and Malcolm X led to Love B. Wood, the proprietor of the Hotel Theresa, agreeing to the successful transfer of the Cuban delegation from the downtown Manhattan hotel to his Harlem home.

Peñalver, we learned, personally interviewed Malcolm X or, as he would tell it, Malcolm "interviewed" him.

In the final analysis, the symposium in itself crystalized Cuba's recognition of Malcolm's contribution to a wave of political thinking and influence which swept not just the United States but the entire world of the 1960s.

This book project became a serious goal from the moment I began editing the conference materials for various radio programs aired over WBAI-Pacifica network in New York.

I knew that those stories had to be told, after witnessing the depth of the Cuban's admiration for Malcolm, exhibited in both the scholarly papers they presented and in listening to the testimonies of those who journeyed with Fidel up to Harlem. Also notable was the interest of Cubans in the street who followed every detail of the symposium which was covered daily in the Havana press.

I then set out to find some of the men and women from this side of the ocean who would compliment the Cubans' memories. Their stories would be an affirmation of the entire episode. This venture proved not so difficult because I went directly to the streets of Harlem — the community I know best. And that is where the history unfurled.

The months of research uncovered a litany of tales and folklore treasured in the memories of old-timers who became my partners in recording *Fidel and Malcolm X: Memories of a meeting.*

The makers of history became the recorders of that history, many having survived the untold pain and injustices of racist

America as African men and women.

Fidel himself, having survived the menacing threats of imperialist aggression, personally gave his own reflections of the meeting with Malcolm X.

As pointed out by the great gentleman of law and struggle, Conrad Lynn, the fact that Fidel is "still there means the option for revolution and change is still present, even for the American people." This book makes an attempt to set the record straight on Fidel's uptown sojourn to the Hotel Theresa. Above all, it recounts Harlem's response to that historic visit which began on September 19, 1960 and ended more than a week later on September 28.

Throughout these pages, the collective voices from both the symposium and the streets of Harlem recapture events where heroes and heroines protected their memories within the bosom of time. These memories I discovered are a real source of hope for the future because they reflect the weapon of truth.

Rosemari Mealy
August 1992
Harlem, New York

Chronology

March 10, 1952
Fulgencio Batista leads a military coup in Cuba, suspends the Constitution, cancels the elections and becomes dictator. The Truman Administration quickly recognizes his government and sends military and economic aid.

July 26, 1953
Fidel Castro and other revolutionaries attack the Moncada military barracks in Santiago de Cuba. Despite the deaths of at least 70 participants and the imprisonment of the rest, including Castro, the July 26 Movement is born from this battle.

May 15, 1955
Responding to a public campaign, General Batista releases Fidel Castro and the other revolutionaries captured in 1953. Castro goes into exile in Mexico and begins to organize an expedition to return to Cuba to launch a revolution.

December 2, 1956
Fidel Castro, his brother Raúl Castro, Ernesto "Che" Guevara, and 79 other revolutionaries aboard the cabin cruiser *Granma* land in Oriente province in Cuba. Most of these guerrillas are soon killed. The survivors establish a base in the Sierra Maestra mountains, working with revolutionaries who have been organizing insurrection inside Cuba.

January 1, 1959
General Fulgencio Batista flees Cuba in the early morning hours. Revolutionary forces led by Fidel Castro assume control in Havana and Santiago de Cuba.

January 7, 1959
The United States recognizes the new Cuban government. Yet, as officially acknowledged many years later, the CIA begins a campaign early in 1959 aimed at overthrowing the Cuban government.

April 15-26, 1959
At the invitation of the Association of Newspaper Editors, Castro makes an unofficial visit to the United States. Greeted wherever he goes by enthusiastic crowds, he tells the Senate Foreign Relations Committee that good relations between the United States and Cuba can only exist on the basis of full equality.

May 17, 1959
Cuban leader Fidel Castro signs the first agrarian reform law, putting a limit on land holdings and expropriating the remainder with compensation to the owners. The land will be distributed among landless Cubans. At the time of the agrarian reform, foreigners owned 75 percent of arable land. Five U.S. sugar companies own or control more than two million acres in Cuba.

1960-61
The United States government imposes an economic blockade of Cuba that is to continue unabated into the 1990s.

Sunday, September 18, 1960
Cuban Premier Fidel Castro arrives in the United States for the 15th Session of the General Assembly of the United Nations. He is greeted at the airport by thousands of well-wishers who follow the Cuban delegation to its hotel. The U.S. government imposes a travel restriction on Castro and the Cuban delegation, forbidding them to move beyond the island of Manhattan in New York. The next day, Castro speaks of the "climate of inhospitality" imposed by the United States government.

Monday, September 19, 1960
After refusing to accept "unreasonable financial demands" by the management of the midtown Shelburne Hotel, Cuba's delegation moves to the Hotel Theresa on 125th Street in Harlem. Thousands crowd the streets to see and cheer them. Fidel Castro and Muslim

leader Malcolm X meet sometime near midnight at the Hotel Theresa.

Tuesday, September 20, 1960
Soviet leader Nikita Khrushchev pays a visit to Fidel Castro at Hotel Theresa.

Wednesday, September 21, 1960
Fair Play for Cuba Committee hosts a reception for Fidel Castro and the Cuban delegation.

Thursday, September 22, 1960
Castro and the Cuban delegation host a luncheon for hotel employees at the Hotel Theresa after being snubbed by U.S. President Dwight D. Eisenhower who held a reception for other Latin American leaders. Premier Castro holds an impromptu news briefing where he tells reporters: "We are not sad. We are going to take it easy. We wish them [Eisenhower and his guests] a good appetite. I will be honored to lunch with the poor and humble people of Harlem. I belong to the poor, humble people."

Friday, September 23, 1960
Premier Castro and the Cuban delegation are guests of Soviet leader Nikita Khrushchev.

Saturday, September 24, 1960
Harlem Branch of Communist Party of the United States, under the leadership of former political prisoner Ben Davis, holds a rally in Harlem in solidarity with Cuba.

Sunday, September 25, 1960
President Gamal Abdel Nassar of the United Arab Republic visits Castro at the Hotel Theresa.

Monday, September 26, 1960
Fidel Castro addresses the UN General Assembly for four and a half hours.

Tuesday, September 27, 1960
Early afternoon, Premier Castro is a guest of President Kwame

Nkrumah of Ghana. At the Hotel Theresa, Castro receives the visit of India's Prime Minister Jawaharlal Nehru and Foreign Minister V.K. Khrisha Menon. He later receives Bulgarian leader Tedor Zhivkov.

Wednesday, September 28, 1960
In the morning, Premier Fidel Castro pays a courtesy call to President Gamal Abdel Nassar of the United Arab Republic. That evening, the Cuban delegation leaves New York and flies back to Havana.

April 17-19, 1961
United States government supports an invasion of Cuba, later known as the Bay of Pigs. Less than 72 hours after the invasion began, Castro announces victory.

October 1962
President Kennedy initiates the "Cuban Missile Crisis", denouncing Cuba's acquisition of missiles capable of carrying nuclear warheads for defense against U.S. attack. Washington imposes a naval blockade on Cuba and threatens the Soviet Union with a nuclear war. Cuba responds by mobilizing its population for defense. On October 28, Soviet Premier Khrushchev agrees to remove the Soviet missiles in exchange for a U.S. pledge not to invade Cuba.

December 13, 1964
Due to threats from right-wing Cuban groups in the United States, Cuban leader Che Guevara, in New York to address the UN General Assembly, is forced to cancel a visit to Harlem to take part in a meeting with Malcolm X. A message from Guevara is read to a public meeting by Malcolm X.

February 21, 1965
Malcolm X is assassinated in Harlem's Audubon Ballroom while addressing a public meeting.

Cuba, Fidel, Harlem and Us

On September 19, 1960, thousands of New Yorkers embraced 125th Street and Seventh Avenue to greet Premier Fidel Castro's arrival. For 24-hours a day, Harlem's streets were carpeted by the energy and warmth of its people. These were rare moments indeed, rivaled only by another event some 30 years later when Nelson Mandela stood almost on the same street corner, looking out over a sea of Black faces cheering his homecoming to the "Black capital of the world."

Bill Epton

It is only fitting and in keeping with the political and historical vanguard role that Harlem held for African Americans and all oppressed people that Fidel Castro should choose it as his base of operations during his historic visit to the United Nations in New York in September 1960.

Beginning with the period after World War I, Harlem became a magnet for the oppressed Black people from the southern states and the Caribbean. Within it, there developed a solid working-class population alongside an intellectual movement deeply rooted in the history, struggles and culture of Africa, the Caribbean and the deep south. Out of this merger developed the period of the Harlem Renaissance — a great flourishing of African American cultural and political enlightenment that shaped our struggle for years to come.

A great mass movement of Black people came into existence during this period, led by Marcus Garvey's Negro Improvement Association, the Communist Party of the USA and some smaller political formations. What they all had in common was a general

14

anti-imperialist position.

They helped to raise the consciousness of the Black masses. Union activities, led by the formation of the CIO (Congress of Industrial Organizations), were taking place all over the country and there was a union consciousness and solidarity that existed in the Harlem community. Into this mix came future African political leaders like Kwame Nkrumah of Ghana and Nnamdi Azekewi of Nigeria and others. It was the people who were born and grew up during this glorious period in our history that formed the backbone of movements that developed during the 1950s and 1960s.

Following World War II, African American soldiers came home with a much different world outlook from when they were drafted. Many left southern plantations and deeply segregated and oppressive lives to find themselves in Asia and Europe "fighting for democracy." Many also became aware of the slogan of the Communist Party, "Victory at home and abroad." In these segregated army units, Blacks from the north and south exchanged experiences, views and ideas on the war at home and abroad. They talked about what life was going to be like once they returned and how they were going to fight for "democracy" in the United States. In addition to the Blacks who were drafted into the army, millions of Blacks were drafted into industry to help feed the war machine. They, too, were politicized in the unions and in the northern communities where industry existed. New York, at that time, was basically an industrialized city.

The U.S. ruling class, responding to developments abroad (revolutions in Europe, national liberation struggles in Asia, Africa and Latin America), launched a counter-attack internationally (the Cold War) and nationally (the anti-communist hysteria in the form of the so-called "McCarthy Period"). This counter-revolution had as its target the trade union movement, the cultural organizations and prominent militant Black leaders. Throughout the south, the U.S. ruling class unleashed the KKK and other pro-fascist and racist groups to attack returning Black soldiers and try to "put them back in their place."

In 1949, just four years after the war to "save democracy," in Clarendon County, South Carolina, some Black cotton and tobacco farmers filed a petition to make their segregated dilapidated school equal to that of the white schools. It was this petition by these heroic Black farmers that led to the Supreme Court decision of 1954 that said these segregated schools were unequal. All over the south and in northern cities struggles like these were taking place — in the courts, in the streets, in factories and in the armed services. The armed forces were desegregated just prior to the war against the Korean people. Black people were marching forward in the face of McCarthyism, the KKK and their allies north and south.

Young heroic African American children and their parents braved racist mobs to fight for a decent education. Many people saw the racist response to these children as not wanting to go to school with Black children. The fundamental issue then, as it is now and as it has always been in this country, is that the ruling class does not want to educate its working class, especially African Americans! But we were not going to be satisfied with what the U.S. ruling class wants — we know what we want and that is our liberation and one of the key battlegrounds in that fight is on the education front!

As the struggle on the education front grew in intensity throughout the south, Black people in northern cities began to realize that in many areas their children were also being shortchanged. Parents in Harlem formed the Harlem Parents Committee to fight for open enrollment, when they realized that in most white communities the public schools were "underutilized" and there was tremendous overcrowding in our schools.

In addition to the struggle around education, many African American heroes and heroines came forth to meet the challenge of those times. Rosa Parks' refusal to give up her seat to a white man on a bus led to the Montgomery Bus Boycott from 1955 to 1959 that was organized by a union man from the Sleeping Car Porters Union. By this time, all over America Black people were on the move. As a result of these pressures from mass struggles, old Jim Crow racist laws and customs began to fall — both legally and under the weight of the people.

The brutal murder of Emmett Till and the student sit-in at a Woolworth lunch counter in Greensboro, North Carolina in early 1960 was of particular importance in the raising of the consciousness of the people of Harlem. Mass rallies in the streets were held to protest the murder of Emmett Till and the people's fightback received new vigor. A. Philip Randolph, the leader of the Sleeping Car Porters Union and other Black trade unionists from across the country issued a call for Black workers to organize and fight against racism and discrimination within the trade union movement. One of the first acts of the emerging New York Chapter of the Negro American Labor Council (NALC) was to form solidarity picket lines and organize boycotts of the Woolworth stores on 125th Street, 116th Street and Lenox Avenue and on 140th Street and Lenox Avenue. The biggest, most massive and most sustained picket was at the 125th Street Woolworth. All over Harlem, organizing was taking place on the education front, on the labor front and in support of our brothers and sisters in the south.

Another important front in our liberation struggle was being led by Jesse Gray, who formed the Lower Harlem Tenants Council to fight with slumlords for decent housing for the working class of Harlem. Jesse Gray was a product and participant of Harlem's militant history, a trade union organizer. Thus, at the beginning of the 1960s all over Harlem, on every front, the people were doing their part in the struggle for our liberation. It should also be noted that it was at this time that the U.S. ruling class massively introduced drugs into the Harlem community!

Some other factors that were at play at that time will help to explain the coming together and warm reception of the people of Harlem and Fidel Castro were:

- the national liberation struggle taking place in Africa, Asia, and Latin America, especially Ghana, which the people of Harlem felt particularly strong about and close to;
- the political work done in our community by Carlos Moore, a Black Cuban, who was a staunch supporter of the Cuban revolution in Harlem, but who later switched sides and became a rabid anti-communist;
- the base of support for the Cuban revolution by Black Cubans, Puerto Ricans and Panamanians who lived in Harlem.

When Malcolm X went to the Hotel Theresa to meet Fidel Castro it was an important and historic meeting, but not the highlight of Castro's visit to Harlem. The meeting attested to the keen sense of history that both of these leaders recognized and their understanding of the oneness of the struggle of the African

American people, the peoples of Asia, Africa, Latin America and particularly Cuba — a country with a large African population. The Nation of Islam was just beginning to make its presence felt in Harlem, primarily through the street sales of its newspaper, *Muhammad Speaks.* Malcolm X at that time was involved chiefly in the internal affairs of the Nation and recruiting new members. Although Malcolm was dedicated to the Nation of Islam, which played a small role up to that time in the Black Liberation movement, he was also a product of the militant energy that was Harlem. Even though the Nation, as an organization, would not participate in the mass struggles that were taking place in Harlem, many of their members, including Malcolm X, understood, sympathized, and felt at one with the masses who were in the streets. It was from within this framework that Malcolm X was moved to pay the historic visit to Fidel Castro.

After Castro and his delegation were insulted by the management of the Shelburne Hotel in midtown Manhattan they moved to the Hotel Theresa, located in Harlem on 125th Street and Seventh Avenue, right around the corner from Woolworth. That move ignited the people of Harlem. Here was a small Caribbean country that had made a revolution and its delegation was coming to the people of Harlem. And here was a community that was totally receptive.

The street corner speakers hailed the move and the revolution and encouraged the people to come out and support the Cuban delegation. Nationalists of all stripes felt as one with their Cuban brothers and sisters. In this symbolic move, the Puerto Rican, Cuban, and Caribbean communities of Harlem saw their salvation and their future. In a matter of hours word spread throughout Harlem and thousands of people were in the streets in front of the Hotel Theresa — from 124th Street to 126th Street — cheering the Cuban delegation. The Harlem welcome committee was almost as large as the welcome committee for Nelson Mandela. It was a great festival of the people. Every time a member of the Cuban delegation came to the hotel window, the masses of people would send up a mighty cheer. No matter who came to the window, the people would say, "There's Castro," and a cheer would go up. This kind of atmosphere lasted as long as the delegation was at the Hotel Theresa. The people were particularly interested in seeing Juan Almeida, the Black member of Castro's delegation and a military hero in Cuba's war of liberation. It seemed as if everyone knew his name and knew about his role and exploits in the revolution. He was our brother and our hero, too! On one of the nights, the Harlem branch of the Communist Party, which had its offices above what was then the Wellworth Tavern, on 126th Street and Seventh Avenue, planned a street rally in support of the revolution and the delegation. An attempt was made to get as close to the hotel as possible to set up the speaker's ladder, but the streets were so crowded with people that the closest the rally could set up was between 126th and 127th Streets on Seventh Avenue. The main speaker at the street meeting was Ben Davis, a Black leader of the Communist Party, who had just been released after five years in jail under the Smith Act. This was the last public street meeting held in Harlem by the Communist Party.

However, the story doesn't end here!

The meeting between Malcolm X and Fidel Castro was not an end in itself. It was at the same time a continuation of the heightened militancy of the African American people of Harlem — and their clear understanding of their position in world history — as well as a milestone in both the lives and development of Malcolm X and Fidel Castro.

For those of us who subsequently met, had conversations with, and came to know Malcolm, it becomes obvious in hindsight that his days in the Nation of Islam were limited. He had a clear understanding of the international situation and the class position of the African American people in the United States. He was able to take great generalities and make them quite specific and show how they applied to our situation. He could sum up complex social, political, and cultural developments in succinct phrases and explain them in clear everyday language that the masses could easily understand. He was politically and intellectually far beyond the myopic outlook of the Nation of Islam.

It was obviously for these reasons that the U.S. ruling class made a decision to remove him from the scene.

But the assassin's bullets were like trying to stop a hurricane with a pistol! The U.S. capitalist rulers may have temporarily diverted our struggles but they know that our struggle is a just one and that we represent the cutting edge as to what direction the United States will take and that we will be victorious in the end. One has to just witness the unparalleled racist onslaught against our people from all levels of the U.S. propaganda machine. This obviously does not come from a ruling class that is secure in its position. It is a display of weakness, not strength! Malcolm X is the symbol of our resistance and fightback, especially among Black youth. It is Malcolm's voice and wisdom that young African Americans are looking for and finding.

Malcolm lives!

And the other party to that meeting — Fidel Castro? There is no speculation as to what has happened over the ensuing 31 years. Cuba has become a shining example of what a free, revolutionary people can do. How they can build a society that fights racism and establishes social, economic, and political justice. Cuba is by far the most advanced country in the western hemisphere in political, cultural, and social development. All of this being achieved while under economic and sometimes military attack from the U.S. government — both Democratic and Republican. These advances were achieved under the leadership of Fidel Castro and the revolutionary leadership of its political party.

So we look back 32 years and remember those eventful days in Harlem. We recall the mood and strength of the people both in Harlem and Havana and we understand the binding ties that unite all oppressed people. We are also keenly aware of how great leaders are able to have profound foresight and understanding of their surroundings. Both Malcolm and Fidel exhibited that keen awareness and the world will be better for it!

Sarah Elizabeth Wright

The raw, gray September day was typical of New York in the fall. But that particular Sunday, September 18, almost 32 years ago, was lit with a unique warmth and excitement. For world leaders were streaming in from all corners of the globe to attend the 1960 UN General Assembly — Nasser, Nehru, Khrushchev and, prompting the greatest excitement in some and the greatest consternation in others, Fidel Castro, not that long from the battlefield, still clad in drab, olive fatigues, coming to give voice to the yearnings of the people of a small island as well as the hopes of the great majority of the world's peoples.

All police leave was cancelled. Some 8,000 cops were mobilized, for there was no telling what the arrival of the bearded leader would precipitate.

Fearful of the virus of freedom, all major white hotels had refused their accommodations to the Cuban entourage. There was no room at the inn, they said, just as the Philistines had advised Mary and Joseph some 2,000 years before. Only after considerable pressure from the UN and the U.S. State Department did the Shelburne Hotel finally consent to admit the Cubans. With these arrangements made, Fidel and his party flew into Idlewild International Airport (now John F. Kennedy).

We who had followed the progress of the Cuban Revolution with growing enthusiasm, we who felt that a piece of ourselves had been liberated when Fidel and his army marched into Havana were glued to the radio, awaiting the announcement of Fidel's arrival.

Thousands went to the airport and then rode back with their Cuban brothers and sisters in an unofficial, people caravan. Thousands converged on the Shelburne, rejoicing, chanting, "Viva Fidel! Viva Cuba!" We thought little of sleep. At home, in the neighborhoods, on the job, we spoke of nothing else.

A night later, the Harlem Writers Guild Workshop met at my home. It was difficult to focus on the work at hand. John Oliver Killens, the great writer and guiding spirit of our Black writers' group, was chairing. Present were John Henrik Clark, later to emerge as one of our most illustrious historians, and a dozen others, then still unknown, but later to be recognized as among the leading figures of Black letters. I myself was in the throes of writing my novel, *This Child's Gonna Live.*

Before our meeting was formally begun, the telephone rang. The caller's news was electrifying. Fidel and the Cuban delegation had left the Shelburne and were proceeding up to the Theresa Hotel in Harlem! Unprecedented! No foreign government leader had ever considered lodging in Harlem to be sufficiently dignified. It was the Harlem to which we affectionately referred as the "Black Capital of the USA"!

Immediately, we scrambled for our coats and headed uptown to cheer Fidel, to make sure no harm befell him. We piled into taxis, jumped out in front of the Hotel Theresa into a mass of humanity buffeted by a driving rain. Rosa Guy, today celebrating the publication of her 20th book, had also joined us by then. Looking up, we could see people crammed onto rooftops, leaning out of thousands of windows. And a steady chanting, "Cuba sí, Yankee no!"

But these were not Cubans. These were my people — the poor, the abused, the disinherited, the trampled leavings of this country, offering their protection and love to the leader of another poor, abused and disinherited people. The streets were packed, but the crowd kept growing, bringing light and warmth to a dark September night, bringing light and warmth into the bleakness of their own lives.

Hundreds of heavily armed police tried to do their intimidating thing — the people did not even notice them.

Shortly after midnight, a roar erupted. Fidel had arrived! We found out later that Malcolm X was the first to greet him. They met on the ninth floor in a suite given to the Cuban leader by Love Woods, a prominent Harlem figure and owner of the hotel.

Fidel told Malcolm X of the incredible inhospitality his party had experienced at the Shelburne, the insulting demand made upon them for a $10,000 deposit against damage to be expected from Cuban "barbarians." He spoke of the "uncivilized and violent" conduct a security guard had accorded him. But above all, he spoke of Harlem.

"I always wanted to come to Harlem," said Fidel, "but I was not sure of what kind of welcome I would get. When I got the news that I would be welcome in Harlem, I was happy." The Black people of the United States were not as brainwashed by the official anti-Cuban propaganda as whites, he continued. And Cuba was wiping out racial discrimination. Cubans, Africans and the Black people of the United States were all in the same boat. "I feel as if I were in Cuba now. I feel very warm here."

Malcolm X responded that it was indeed true that, "We in Harlem are not addicted to all the propaganda they [the U.S. government] put out." And then they embraced.

Immediately thereafter, world leaders, including Nikita Khrushchev, made their pilgrimages to the Hotel Theresa to greet Fidel Castro. For a brief period, Harlem became a world capital, much to Washington's embarrassment.

Several days later, upon Fidel's invitation, I along with hundreds of others, came up to the Theresa to embrace him, to embrace Cuba, and to embrace revolution.

Fidel Castro

Addressing the UN on September 26, Fidel Castro outlined the "problem of Cuba," and why the example of a tiny island excited such a response on the streets of Harlem.

The problem of Cuba. Perhaps some of you may be well aware of the facts; others, perhaps, may not – it all depends on the sources of information. As far as the world is concerned the problem of Cuba has come to a head – it has appeared in the last two years and as such it is a new problem. The world had not had many reasons to know that Cuba existed. For many it was an off-shoot of the United States. And this is the case for many citizens of this very country – Cuba was virtually a colony of the United States. As far as the map was concerned, the map said something different. Cuba was colored differently from the color that was used for the United States; but in reality Cuba was a colony of the United States....

Colonies do not speak. Colonies are not recognized in the world. Colonies are not allowed to express their opinions until they are granted permission to do so. That is why our colony and its problems were unknown to the rest of the world.... Let no one be mistaken. There was no independent republic. It was a colony where orders were given by the Ambassador of the United States of America. We are not ashamed of proclaiming this from the rooftops. On the contrary: we are proud that we can say today that no embassy rules our people; our people are governed by Cuba's people.

Once again, the Cuban people had to turn and fight to achieve independence and that independence was finally attained after seven bloody years of tyranny. What tyranny? The tyranny of those who in our country were nothing but the cat's-paws of those who dominated our country economically....

It was the type of government of force – that of Fulgencio Batista – that was most appropriate for the United States monopolies in Cuba, but that was not the type of government that was appropriate for the Cuban people. Therefore, the Cuban people, squandering life, rose up and threw that government out. And, when the revolution was successful in Cuba, what did it uncover? What marvels lay spread out before the eyes of the victorious revolutionaries of Cuba? First of all, the revolution found that 600,000 Cubans, able and ready to work, were unemployed – as many, proportionally, as were unemployed in the United States at the time of the Great Depression which shook this country and which almost produced a catastrophe in the United States. This is what we met with – permanent unemployment in my country. Three million out of a population of somewhat over six million had no electric light and none of the advantages and comforts of electricity. Three and a half million out of a total population of more than six million lived in huts, in slums, without the slightest sanitary facilities. In the cities, rents took almost one-third of family incomes. Electricity rates and rents were among the highest in the world.

Thirty-seven and one-half percent of our population were illiterate; 70 percent of the rural children lacked teachers; 2 percent of our population suffered from tuberculosis, that is to say, one hundred thousand persons, out of a total population of a little over six million, were suffering from the ravages of tuberculosis. Ninety-five percent of the children in rural areas were suffering from parasites. Infant mortality was astronomical. The standard of living was the opposite. On the other hand, 85 percent of the small farmers were paying rent on their land to the extent of almost 30 percent of their gross income, whilst 1.5 percent of the total landowners controlled 46 percent of the total area of the country. Of course, the proportion of hospital beds to the number of inhabitants of the country was ludicrous when compared with countries that have even half-way decent medical services. Public services, electricity and telephone services all belonged to United States monopolies. A major portion of the banking business, of importing business and the oil refrineries, a greater part of the sugar production, the lion's share of the arable land of Cuba and the most important industries in all fields in Cuba belonged to North American companies.

The balance of payments in the last 10 years, from 1950 to 1960, has been favorable for the United States vis-a-vis Cuba to the extent of one billion dollars. This is without taking into account the hundreds of millions of dollars that were extracted from the treasury of the country by the corrupt officials of the tyranny and were later deposited in United States or European banks. One billion dollars in 10 years! The poor and underdeveloped country in the Caribbean, with 600,000 unemployed, was contributing to the economic development of the most highly industrialized country in the world!

This was the situation that confronted us. Yet it should not surprise many of the countries represented in this Assembly, because, when all is said and done, what we have said about Cuba is, one may say, an X-ray that could be superimposed and applied to many of the countries here represented in the Assembly....

What has the revolutionary government done? What is the crime committed by the revolutionary government, for it to be pilloried -- as it has been here -- for it to find itself confronted by as powerful an enemy as has been shown us to have? Did the problems with the United States government come up at the first moment? No. When we came to power, were we posessed with the desire to find international difficulties? No. We did not pause to consider international problems. No revolutionary government achieving power wants international problems. What it wants to do is devote itself to the settling of its own problems at home; to carry out a program for the betterment of the people, as all governments do that are truly concerned with the progress of their country.

The first unfriendly act perpetrated by the government of the United States was to throw open its doors to a gang of murderers, bloodthirsty criminals. Men who had murdered hundreds of defenseless peasants, who had never tired of torturing prisoners for many, many years, who had killed right and left. These hordes were received by this country with open arms. We were deeply amazed. Why this unfriendly act on the part of the government of the United States towards Cuba? Why this act of hostility? At that time we could not quite understand. Now we see clearly the reasons.

Was the policy a correct treatment of Cuba? Is Cuba being punished? But the injured party is Cuba. We were the injured party, because the government of Batista was kept in power with the assistance of tanks, planes and weapons supplied by the government of the United States.

The system of Batista's government was kept in power thanks to the use of an army, the officers of which were instructed and trained by a military mission of the United States government. We trust that no official of the United States will dare to deny that fact and that truth....

So the revolutionary government began to take the first steps. The first was the 50 percent reduction in rents paid by families -- a very just measure since, as I said earlier, there were families paying up to one-third of their incomes for rent.... Then another law was passed, a law cancelling the concessions which had been granted by the tyranny of Batista to the telephone company which was a United States monopoly.... The third measure was the reduction of the cost of electricity, which had been one of the highest in the world.... Then followed another law, an essential law, inevitable as far as our own people were concerned, and a law which, sooner or later, will be passed all over the world. This was the agrarian reform law.

In our country such reform was inevitable. More than 200,000 peasant families lived in the country without land upon which to plant the essential foodstuffs. Without agrarian reform our country could not have taken its first tottering steps towards development, but we were able finally to take that step. We instituted an agrarian reform. Was it radical? It was a radical reform. Was it very radical? It was not very radical. We instituted an agrarian reform adjusted to the needs of our development, adjusted to the possibilities of agricultural development, that is, an agrarian reform that would solve the problems of the landless peasants, that would solve the problem of the lack of basic foodstuffs, that would solve the great unemployment problem on the land, that would end, once and for all, the ghastly misery which existed in the rural areas of our country.

And that is where the first major difficulty arose....

Then the question of payments and indemnities came up. Notes from the State Department rained on Cuba. They never asked us about our problems, not even out of a desire to express condolence or commiseration, or because of the hand that they had had in creating the problems....

Can you gentlemen conceive how a poor, underdeveloped country carrying the onus of 600,000 unemployed, with such a high numbe. of sick and illiterate, whose reserves have been sapped, that has contributed to the economy of a powerful country to the tune of one billion dollars in 10 years, can have the wherewithall to pay for the lands that are going to be affected by the agrarian reform, c ˙ at least pay for them on the conditions on which the North American State Department wanted to be paid in compensation for their affected interests?

We were not 150 percent communists at that time. We just appeared slightly pink. We were not confiscating lands. We simply proposed to pay for them in 20 years, and the only way in which we could pay for them was by bonds – bonds which would mature in 20 years, at 4.5 percent interest, which would accumulate annually.

How were we to be able to pay for these lands in dollars? How were we going to pay in cash, on the spot, and how could we pay for them what they asked? It was ludicrous.

It is obvious that under those circumstances we had to choose between carrying through an agrarian reform and nothing. If we chose nothing then there would be a perpetuation of the economic misery of our country, and if we did carry out the agrarian reform then we were exposing ourselves to incurring the hatred of the government of the powerful neighbor of the north. We went ahead with the agrarian reform....

The attitude of the revolutionary government already had been too bold. It had clashed with the interests of the international telephone trust; it had clashed with the interests of the international mining trusts; it had clashed with the interests of the United Fruit Company and it had clashed, virtually, with the most powerful interests of the United States, which, as you know, are very closely linked one with the other. And that was more than the government of the United States could tolerate – that is, the representatives of the United States' monopolies.

But the interests which were affected by the Cuban revolution were not concerned over the case of Cuba; they were not being ruined by the measures of the Cuban revolutionary government. That was not the problem. The problem lay in the fact that these same interests owned the natural wealth and resources of the greater part of the peoples of the world.

So then the example shown by the Cuban revolution had to receive its punishment. Punitive actions of every type – even the destruction of Cuba's foolhardy people – had to be carried out against the audacity of the revolutionary government....

Those are the circumstances in which the revolutionary process in Cuba has taken place.... What was yesterday a hopeless land, a land of misery, a land of illiterates, is gradually becoming one of the most enlightened, advanced and developed lands of this continent.

Elombe Brath
Patrice Lumumba Coalition

It was after coming in contact with the Nation of Islam (NOI) and its leader Elijah Muhammad that Malcolm began his rise as the sharp tongued, fiery orator that would cast him in the national spotlight as Mr. Muhammad's representative and the role of Black leader. Arriving in New York in 1954 — the same year as the Supreme Court's monumental decision outlawing separate but equal education and a year before Dr. Martin Luther King, Jr. launched the Montgomery bus boycott and the Bandung conference of African-Asian nations was held in Indonesia — Malcolm would become juxtaposed to the civil rights leader, representing the polarization between two points in the Black freedom struggle that compete for the minds, hearts and souls of our people for at least the next decade.

The Africentric character that would distinguish Malcolm's rhetorical style and his denunciation of Eurocentric values that had been imposed upon the Black community after three centuries of brainwashing would pose his view as an alternative to the passive nature of the civil rights movement. But what made Malcolm such an important figure in the Black Muslim movement, lifting him above all Muslim ministers representing Mr. Muhammad was the fact that when Malcolm arrived in Harlem to take charge of Mosque #7 he did not step into a vacuum. Indeed, he quickly became part of a community which had developed a strong Black nationalist tradition from its inception.

Historically, Harlem had been viewed all over the world as the "Capital of Black America." It is a community that has also been the soul of African nationalism in the United States since it was the headquarters of the Garvey movement around 1918. The Nation of Islam was founded in the Midwest as an eclectic, ecclesiastical messianic movement based on a fundamental Black nationalist idea with the adaptation of some essential features of Islam (similar to its predecessor the Moorish Temple of Science led by Noble Drew Ali). Masonic codes and old fashion Baptist "call and response" type mass meetings. Its ultimate goal was the development of a theocratic Black nation state, either in the United States or somewhere else. It was not African-oriented in the true sense of African nationalism, as we understand that concept today. In fact, the Nation of Islam rejected even the term Africa, seeing the African continent as East Asia — an outlook that defied geography as well as history — and saw "the so-called Negro" as Asiatic, Black men and Black women.

Known formally as the *Lost-Found Nation of Islam in the Wilderness of North America*, the group believed that the white man was a devil that was created by a deranged Black scientist name Yacub causing our people to be cursed by Allah, and that there was an interplanetary spaceship — entitled the Mothership — with brothers from another planet that would intervene when the word was given and destroy our oppressors. There was also a fixed pre-intervene of time for our subjugation (of several thousand years) before our freedom could be obtained. This was the teaching of all Nation of Islam mosques or temples throughout the country and was dictated as Holy Writ in their journal, *The Supreme Wisdom*. That was until Malcolm arrived in Harlem.

Booker Johnson
member of the Nation of Islam

The year 1960 was the peak of the street speakers in Harlem. You had [James Rupert] Lawson [presiding elder of the United African National Movement], [Edward] Davis, Malcolm X and Carlos Cooks — they were the pioneers, they were the cornerstone up there on that corner at 125th and Seventh Avenue [referring also to the site of the Theresa Hotel], and Chock Full O'Nuts Restaurant was their United Nations. These leaders had studied. Many of them had been incarcerated by the power structure. They knew what they wanted to do. They had a plan — that is why they were successful.

Elombe Brath

It was the preponderance of Black nationalist street corner speakers that changed Malcolm's modus operandi of promoting the Nation of Islam's tenets. First, as has been documented by D.E.U. Essien-Udon, professor of history at the University of Ibadan in Nigeria, Malcolm initiated the move to adopt the street corner rallies like the Garveyite Black nationalist instead of strictly holding meetings in the temples like most Black religious institutions. He also started to speak more about Africa, acknowledging Garvey's influence, encouraging self-determination and criticizing the goals, tactics and strategies of the civil rights movement personified by Dr. King, Roy Wilkins of the NAACP, Whitney Young of the Urban League and James Farmer of the Congress of Racial Equality.

In adapting a Black nationalist position the greatest influence that Malcolm fell under was that of Carlos A. Cooks, the Dominican Republic-born Garveyite who was the founder and first administrator of the African Nationalist Pioneer Movement

(ANPM)... founded a year after Garvey's death in 1941 and the first self-professed African nationalist organization known in the United States.

Contrary to what has been generally accepted, most of the concepts and symbols that would characterize Black nationalism in the 1960s and be identified with Malcolm X were in reality initiated by Mr. Cooks. These included the 1959 Convention to abrogate the word Negro as the official racial classification of Black people and replace the term with African when speaking of land origin, heritage and national identity (irrespective of birthplace) and the proud usage of Black, when dealing with color (in spite of complexion)....

It should be noted that the year 1959 was a very important year for ideas expressed in this symposium since it was the eve of the 1960s and shaped a lot of its motion. First of all, in my estimate, the 1959 Convention was possibly the most important meeting, a catalyst, that (with the exception of Dr. Essien-Udom) most students and professors of the contemporary Black liberation movement in the United States tend to overlook. It is important for a number of reasons, among which are the facts that (1) it occurred *seven months after the triumph of the Cuban Revolution;* (2) it laid the foundation for the Black consciousness and African cultural movement of the period; (3) it sharpened the contradictions between the Black nationalist and civil rights movements; (4) it also took a strong position of developing a material support network to aid the fledging African nationalist struggles in Africa; and (5) it was the year when the media launched a massive attack on Black nationalism with the CBS Mike Wallace television program entitled "The Hate That Hate Produced."

It was this program — The Hate That Hate Produced — that thrust Malcolm X into the homes and consciousness of white America, projecting Black militants not as legitimate spokespersons for the aspirations, national identity and proponents of self-determination but as embittered, irresponsible Black "racists," reacting wildly to white racism. This production established a pattern by the state to poison the atmosphere for Black radicalism in general and Malcolm in particular for getting a fair hearing from the viewers.... The state's strategy, however, backfired. This happened when millions of Black people, many for the first time, saw a Black man ridiculing white racism... extolling African historical achievements and presenting a bold, assertive and defiant image instead of a passive, begging-oriented philosophy as promoted by civil rights activists.

It is clear to many of us that a concerted effort was made to promote the Nation as a bogeyman threat if entrenched white racism did not allow the reform advocated by the civil rights movement to take place. While Malcolm as an individual was developing as an anti-imperialist champion, he boldly met with Premier Fidel Castro when the Cuban leader stayed at the Hotel Theresa in Harlem, arguing a class analysis in non-Marxist terms (that is, the *field* Negro versus the *house* Negro). The Nation was viewed as pro-capitalist and virtually nonconfrontational in both the domestic arena and on the international scene.

Malcolm's brilliance as a Harlem street corner orator captured the hopes of his audience as he offered them not only an analysis but also preached a program of action.

He argued that the political policies of the United States were linked to the worldwide struggle against colonialism and imperialism. In simple terms, he could dissect the cause of hunger suffered by the children in the ghettos of the United States and the indignation experienced by the dispossessed who lived in the rat-infested flats of urban America, and relate it to the suffering of their counterparts in Asia, Latin American and Africa.

He taught that the same culprit of greed was responsible for stripping away the humanity of the oppressed all over the world.

Malcolm's oratory and popularity among the street masses also won him respect from the broader ideological components of the Black liberation movement. When Malcolm addressed the plight of Black people in their struggle against racism, for human rights and an end to the naked violence perpetuated by the state against their communities, he was also speaking in the context of an evolving consensus among many other African American organizations.

He placed world events, including the Cuban revolution, in the context of people struggling against the dominant ideology of racism.

From the Shelburne to the Theresa

When the Cuban delegation arrived in New York in September 1960 for the 15th session of the UN General Assembly, the revolution was only one year old. Despite its youth, the administration of Dwight Eisenhower along with counter-revolutionary Cubans had already decided on a policy of hostility toward the newly independent country and its leader, Fidel Castro.

Fidel had visited the United States in 1959. Eisenhower, the former general-elected president, refused even to meet the young leader, despite the fact that he had been invited by the Overseas Press Club. Richard Nixon, who was then vice-president, interviewed Fidel, and concluded — according to Raúl Roa — "that [Fidel] was either very naive or he was a communist. That is what Nixon wrote on a piece of paper to the President, and as of that moment, a determined policy against the Cuban revolution was adopted by the United States," Roa recalls.

As the time for the UN assembly drew nearer, Dr. Manuel Bisbé Alberni, who at the time held the title of Cuban Ambassador Extraordinary and Plenipotentiary, Permanent Representative to the United Nations, began scouting around for hotel accommodation for the Prime Minister and his delegation. The Ambassador had suggested that the delegates be lodged at the Waldorf Astoria Hotel, where many of the other heads of state were staying. Raúl Roa Kouri, the youngest envoy of the diplomatic corp, disagreed with the senior diplomat's choice of the Waldorf being the most suitable place for Fidel. Dr. Bisbé eventually agreed with Roa and together they proceeded to look for other hotels.

Even before the arrival of the Cuban delegation in the United States, Roa Kouri had already spoken to Bob Taber of the Fair Play for Cuba Committee about possible hotel accommodation in a "forbidden" part of town. Taber, who was a founding member of the Committee, informed Roa that Malcolm X had already been contacted. Roa remembers Taber telling him that "Malcolm had already suggested that we use the Hotel Theresa in Harlem." Roa began to advance the idea to his delegation that the Cubans should take shelter in Harlem, arguing that their presence would represent the convergence of the Black and Hispanic world. At that time, mention of the Third World was not made. In Roa's opinion, the Cubans' presence in Harlem would seal a bond between those who had struggled and won their liberation, while being in the midst of those whose struggle was taking on a definitive mood and form against racial and economic oppression. Unfortunately, by the time the young diplomat arrived back at the Cuban Mission, he was informed that the Shelburne Hotel had been selected to house the delegation. At the time, the Shelburne Hotel was located near the then Cuban Consulate on East 44th Street. Having failed to convince his associates to relocate uptown, Raúl Roa shelved the idea for future reference — just in case.

The day of Fidel's arrival, the 34-year-old head of state was greeted by cheering crowds of patriotic Cubans. They lined the airport route. A reactionary group of Cuban exiles who called themselves Rosa Blanca (White Rose) formed a picket line in front of the Shelburne. These U.S.-inspired exiles were separated from the hotel by a line of police, having already embarked on a dangerous campaign of terrorism in threatening to blow up the hotel.

On Monday, September 19, the second day of the delegation's stay, the hotel management, represented by Dan Grad, requested a meeting with a representative of the Prime Minister. Fidel asked Raúl Roa if he would meet with the manager, as he was one of the few members of the delegation who spoke English.

Raúl Roa Kouri

The manager said, "Look Mr. Roa, my hotel is running a great risk. There are hoards of people who are threatening to create disorders, to throw rocks against my hotel, and to provoke a great deal of damage.... I want you to inform your Prime Minister that he must deposit a $20,000 security fee in order to stay in my hotel." I told the manager, "I don't think that will be possible, but I will convey the message."

When Fidel was told what the manager had said his immediate response was one of outrage, labelling the Shelburne manager a "gangster"... "How can he ask for a $20,000 deposit?" said Fidel. "That's a problem for the New York police. They are the ones who have to maintain order."

I then went back to the manager and told him what Fidel had

said: that he refused to pay that amount, not even a single dollar.
Fidel had also insisted that I tell the manager to his face that he
was a gangster. So, I went back downstairs and I said,"Look, the
Prime Minister says that you are a gangster, and that he is not
going to pay $20,000 and that you are simply mistaken, we are not
going to pay a single cent."

The manager then told Roa they were evicted from the hotel. Roa
returned to Fidel, where he relayed the manager's message. The
Prime Minister then told the delegation, "We are leaving
immediately." In the September 20, 1960 issue of the *New York
Times*, Grad was quoted as saying: "There was no cash problem
involved. We're not worried about money."

Fidel was livid as he prepared to depart the Shelburne for a
meeting at the United Nations with Secretary-General Dag
Hammarskjold, where he was to denounce the U.S. government for
the despicable treatment the delegation had received from the
moment they had arrived in the United States. And now, this final
straw — the Shelburne attempt to extort $20,000, or "unacceptable
cash demands" as the papers then reported. In the event that the
Secretary-General would not intervene in this matter of diplomacy,
Fidel had already started preparing for a showdown which could
prove to be a very embarrassing matter for the United Nations. The
Cubans were preparing to take things into their own hands to solve
their accommodation problems.

Fidel had asked Dr. Núñez Jiménez, who was the executive
director of the National Institute of Agrarian Reform and another
member of the delegation, to go to an army and navy store to
purchase tents. "We're going to put up tents outside the United
Nations," Fidel told everybody.

Raúl Roa Kouri

We were all in Fidel's room before we were to depart the hotel. I
recall that there were two beds in the room and we were all sitting
there while Fidel was walking from one end of the room to the next.
I recalled that my father, Comrade Raúl Roa, who was then Cuban
foreign minister, was sitting in front of me. I reached down and said
to him, "I have a hotel where Fidel can go," and he said, "Which
hotel?" "The Theresa Hotel," I replied. "Which one is that," my
father asked? "The one in Harlem," I said. "Why didn't you say
so?" he asked me. I responded, "Because they had selected this
hotel and because the chief had decided that Fidel should be

lodged here and a contract had been signed." My father then said, "Well that's over. Tell Fidel about your idea." So while Fidel continued to walk from one side of the room to the other, I said, "Fidel, I have a hotel." He didn't pay any attention whatsoever to what I was saying because he was thinking about going to the UN and talking to Hammarskjold in order to denounce the situation. But I insisted. I said, "Fidel, I have a hotel." "What? Which hotel?" he asked. "The Hotel Theresa." "Where is this hotel?" "It's in Harlem." Then, Fidel repeated, "In Harlem?... In the ghetto? In the Black ghetto?" "Yes," I said. He then asked whether I could get us rooms. I told him I was certain of it. He again asked me how and I explained, "Through Malcolm X." Fidel then asked how I knew Malcolm and I told him about Bob Taber. Fidel then said, "Go get Taber and then go see Malcolm X. And book the Theresa Hotel!" Fidel then left for the United Nations. That's how it happened.

Raúl Roa was not present, however, when the two leaders met.

Conrad Lynn
longtime activist and attorney
Fidel, as a head of state, was not comfortable at the Shelburne Hotel. He didn't like it there. One of the ways that they tried to ridicule the delegation in the press was to claim that they were being evicted because they had live chickens in their rooms. I don't know if that was true or not, and even if it was, it could have been a custom. I had lawyer friends in Puerto Rico who kept live chickens in their offices, because when they ate chicken, they wanted fresh chicken [chuckle]. So if it was a custom in Puerto Rico, it may have been a custom in Cuba, too.

Fidel wanted to move away from there — in fact, he wanted to go to Harlem.

I was a member of the Fair Play for Cuba Committee and a friend of Bob Taber. Taber had phoned me a few days before Fidel arrived in the United States. Taber told me that he expected that there might be "some difficulties at the downtown hotel." My next door neighbor, Jim Dixon, started casting around for another place. Jim had the happy inspiration to suggest that I call the Hotel Theresa in Harlem to ask about accommodation for the Cuban delegation. So I got in touch with the manager, Love Woods, who I knew well. He was hesitant at first, it being a Saturday night. He said, "Look Lynn, I don't think his [Fidel's] check is going to be cashable around here, and the only way that I am going to let him in here is if you get the cash in advance..." He said he would need $900.

As I told you before, I had done a lot of criminal law, so I knew a lot of the big gangsters and the big gamblers. It came to me that gamblers would have that kind of money on a weekend, so I contacted a sympathetic gambler. I went to one of them big gangsters and I said, I need cash! I don't remember how much it was, maybe a thousand dollars. The gambler gave it to me. He didn't say that he was a communist, he didn't say that he was politically developed, but something told me that this was a man, and that he wanted to help. *Did you hear me?* So, the gambler put up the thousand bucks. He was Black, and I gave it over to Mr. Love. [Attorney Lynn would not divulge the name of this mysterious benefactor.]

The money was paid, and around midnight on Monday, September 19, Fidel and the Cuban delegation checked into Love B. Woods' Hotel Theresa in Harlem.

Booker Johnson
Nation of Islam

The government dispossessed Fidel from downtown and they even tried to put pressure on Mr. Woods. That's the reason that I know Mr. Woods had respect for Black folk, 'cause the government tried to force him from letting Castro in. But he told the government that it was a public hotel and they couldn't dictate who he rented the rooms in his hotel to.

Love was a highly educated man, but he was also a hustler — he loved the idea of Fidel coming to stay in his hotel.

Conrad Lynn

Mr. Love made it plain to me that he did not want to become involved politically. He was going to give him the hospitality of the hotel, but he wanted it to be known that he did it purely as the proprietor of the hotel, and that he was not making an endorsement of Fidel's position. He made that very clear and he told me that he would appreciate it if I let that be known.

The news that the Cuban delegation was moving to a Harlem hotel was not well received by UN chief Dag Hammarskjold. Besides, Hammarskjold was in a panic that the Cubans might make real their threat to actually camp out on the grounds of the United Nations. What an embarrassment that would be! Word was already out that the Cubans were either heading for Harlem, or they were planning to pitch tents on the UN grounds. No doubt the Secret Service was getting anxious because, right in the midst of the whole episode, the Cubans started receiving calls from the best hotels in town, offering suites and entire floors, free of charge. Fidel told Hammarskjold that they were not going to accept the new offers because they had already booked the Hotel Theresa in Harlem. They would be heading uptown immediately. Dave Silver was a young school teacher in Harlem. On his way home, he stopped off at the Chock Full O'Nuts on 125th Street for a quick bite. As he sat at the counter eating a hamburger, he saw crowds moving west on to Seventh Avenue. He remembers it as one of the biggest outpourings of people that he had ever seen in his life.

Preston Wilcox
Harlem activist and founder of the Malcolm X Lovers Network

The Hotel will always be a landmark because of Castro's visit. During the Premier's stay in Harlem, Nikita Khrushchev, Abdel Nasser and a many others came up to Harlem. What I recall most vividly were the Black Cubans who were on the side of the street where the hotel was and those Cubans who were opposing him, who looked more white. They were across the opposite street.

When Fidel came to Harlem, it gave many of us a sense that Harlem had a vanguard role in reshaping the world.

[Fidel was one of the first international leaders to set foot on Harlem soil, particularly in such] a very public way. Fidel's visit to Harlem marked the beginning of a new era. It's interesting that he arrived in the early morning on September 20, 1960, on a Tuesday, and the essential revolution of Black people in the United States against their oppression was precipitated in the 1960s. It was like a spiritual connection.

Many observers of Fidel's visit to Harlem say that it made this country more wary of the fraternal ties which can become a reality through struggle. The FBI and CIA activities were stepped up during this period, not only because Fidel was in the United States, but because he met with a local leader.

Fidel Castro

Fidel was delighted in the astuteness of his young diplomat whom he credits with maneuvering the now historic hotel switch to Harlem.

We had two choices. One was the United Nations gardens — when I mentioned this to the Secretary-General, he was horrified at the thought of a delegation camping there in tents. But when we received Malcolm X's offer — he had spoken with one of our comrades — I said, "That is the place, the Hotel Theresa." And there we went.

In his opening remarks to the General Assembly of the United Nations on September 26, 1960, Fidel Castro made these observations:

Some people may think that we are very annoyed and upset by the treatment that the Cuban delegation has received. This is not the case. We understand full well the reason for the state of things. That is why we are not irritated. Nor need anyone concern themselves that Cuba will spare any effort to bring about an understanding in the world. But of this you may be sure, we will speak frankly.

It is extremely expensive to send a delegation to the United Nations. We of the underdeveloped countries do not have too many resources to squander, and when we do spend money in this fashion it is because we wish to speak frankly in this meeting of the representatives of practically all the countries of the world.

The speakers who preceded me here on this rostrum have expressed their concern as regards the problems that are of interest to the whole world. We too are concerned with the same problems. However, in the case of Cuba a special circumstance exists, and that is that Cuba, as far as the world today is concerned, must itself be a preoccupation because different speakers who have spoken here quite correctly have said that among the problems at present facing the world there is the problem of Cuba.

And that is a fact. Apart from the problems that concern the world today, Cuba has problems that concern Cuba itself, problems that worry our people. Much has been said of the world desire for peace — that is the desire of all people and, as such, it is also the desire of our people. But this peace that the world wishes to preserve is the peace which we, the Cubans, have not been able to count upon for a long time. The dangers which other peoples of the world may now consider more or less far removed are problems and preoccupations that for us are very near and close. It has not been easy to come here to this Assembly and to talk about the problems of Cuba; it has not been easy for us to come here. I do not know whether you are privileged in this respect. Are we, the Cuban delegation, the representatives of the type of government that you would call the worst in the world? Do we, the Cuban delegation, warrant and deserve the bad treatment that we have received? And why has our delegation been singled out? Cuba has sent many delegations to the United Nations. Cuba has been represented in the United Nations by many different persons — yet it was we who were singled out for such exceptional measures: confinement to the island of Manhattan; notice to all hotels not to rent rooms to us; hostility; and under the pretext of security, isolation.

Perhaps none of you, upon arrival in the city of New York, has had to suffer the personal mistreatment, the physically humiliating treatment, as that which was meted out to the president of the Cuban delegation.

I am not trying to arouse anyone in this Assembly. I am merely stating the truth. It was time for us to take the floor and to speak. Much has been said about us. For many days we have been a bone of contention. The newspapers have referred to us, but we have held our peace. We cannot defend ourselves against attacks in this country, but our day to tell the truth has dawned and, therefore, we will speak.

As I have said, we have had to undergo degrading and humiliating treatment including eviction from the hotel in which we were living. We headed towards another hotel, without upsets on our part, and we did all in our power to avoid difficulties. We refrained from leaving our hotel rooms and we went nowhere except to this assembly hall of the United Nations on the few times we have come to the General Assembly. We also accepted an invitation to a reception at the Soviet Embassy, but we have curtailed our movements in order to avoid difficulties and problems. Yet, this did not suffice; this did not mean that we were left in peace.

When we were forced to leave one of the hotels of this city and were coming to the United Nations Headquarters while other efforts were being made, a humble hotel of this city, a hotel of the

Negroes of Harlem, took us in....

The reply came as we were speaking to the Secretary-General. Nevertheless, an official of the [U.S.] State Department did all in his power to try to stop us from being given rooms in the hotel. But, at that moment, as though magically, hotels began springing up all over New York. Hotels which had previously refused to grant us rooms now offered to give us rooms — even for nothing. But we, out of elementary courtesy, accepted the offer of the hotel in Harlem. We felt then that we had earned the right to peace and quiet. But no, this was not granted to us.

Since nobody could stop us from living in Harlem, the campaigns of slander and defamation had already begun. The news was put around that the Cuban delegation had found itself a home in a brothel. For some, a humble hotel in Harlem, a hotel inhabited by the Negroes of the United States, must be a brothel.

Were we of the caliber of men that we are described as, then imperialism would not have lost hope, as it has lost hope long ago, of buying us or of seducing us in some way. But, since for a long time imperialism has lost hope of getting us back and it never had a right to hope so — affirming that the Cuban delegation had taken rooms in a brothel they should recognize the fact that imperialist finance capital is a prostitute that cannot seduce us — and it is not necessarily the "respectful prostitute" of Jean Paul Sartre.

"When he stepped out of the car and was whisked quickly into the unpretentious aging Theresa, smack in the center of Harlem, a roar of welcome went up. 'We want Castro,' chanted the crowd."

New York Citizen-Call, September 24, 1960

Going upstairs — Malcolm X greets Fidel

Only three newsmen were allowed into the historic meeting which took place between Malcolm X and Fidel.

Within an hour of Fidel's arrival, African American reporters Jimmy Booker of the *Amsterdam News*, Ralph D. Matthews of the *New York Citizen-Call*, and photojournalist Carl Nesfield were whisked past hundreds of reporters representing major news media from all over the country to the ninth floor of the hotel.

New York Citizen-Call
by Ralph D. Matthews
September 24, 1960

To see Premier Fidel Castro after his arrival at Harlem's Hotel Theresa meant getting past a small army of New York City policeman guarding the building, and past security officers, U.S. and Cuban.

But one hour after the Cuban leader's arrival, Jimmy Booker of the *Amsterdam News*, photographer Carl Nesfield and myself were huddled in the stormy petrel of the Caribbean's room listening to him trade ideas with Muslim leader Malcolm X.

Dr. Castro did not want to be bothered with reporters from the other daily newspapers, but he did consent to see two

41

representatives from the Negro press.

Malcolm X gained entry when few others could because he had recently been named to a welcoming committee for visiting dignitaries set up by Harlem's 28th Police Precinct Council.

We followed Malcolm and his aides, Joseph and John X down the ninth floor corridor. It was lined with photographers, disgruntled because they had no glimpse of the bearded Castro, and writers vexed because security men kept pushing them back.

We brushed by them, and one by one were admitted to Dr. Castro's suite. He rose and shook hands with each one of us in turn. He seemed in a fine mood. The rousing Harlem welcome still seemed to ring in his ears.

Castro was dressed in green army fatigues. I expected them to be as sloppy as news photos tended to make. To my surprise, his casual attire, just the same was immaculately creased and spanking clean.

His beard by dim room light was dark brown with just a suggestion of red.

After introductions, he sat on the edge of the bed, bade Malcolm X sit beside him and spoke in his curious brand of broken English. His first words were lost to us assembled around him. But Malcolm heard him and answered, "Downtown for you, it was ice, uptown it is warm."

The Premier smiled appreciatively. "Aahh yes, we feel very warm here."

Then the Muslim leader, ever a militant, said, "I think you will find the people in Harlem are not so addicted to the propaganda they put out downtown."

In halting English, Dr. Castro said, "I admire this. I have seen how it is possible for propaganda to make changes in people. Your people live here and are faced with this propaganda all the time and yet, they understand. This is very interesting."

"There are 20 million of us," said Malcolm X, "and we always understand."

Members of the Castro party spilled over from an adjoining room, making the small quarters even more cramped. Most of the Cubans smoked long cigars and when something amused them, they threw their heads back and blew smoke puffs as they laughed.

Castro's conversational gestures were unusual. He would touch his temples with extended fingers as he made a point of tapping his chest as if to see if they were still there.

Fidel Castro and Malcolm X, September 19, 1960

New York police (above) mobilizing outside Shelburne Hotel on September 18, 1960, and (below) Cuban delegation leaving the Shelburne Hotel the next day

Outside the Hotel Theresa

EXCLUSIVE MIDNIGHT INTERVIEW WITH FIDEL

SEE PAGE 5

ADAM TO STUMP FOR KENNEDY

SEE PAGE 3

CABBIE FREED IN 'RAG DOLL' DEATH CASE

SEE PAGE 5

Conn. Mother Fights Return To Dixie

SEE PAGE 5

Cuba's Castro Meets Harlem's Malcolm X Shortly After Premier's Arrival At Hotel Theresa. See Exclusive Story, Page 5. Exclusive Photo — Nesfield.

New York Citizen-Call, September 24, 1960

Fidel Castro (above) in lobby of Hotel Theresa and (below) Juan
Almeida in Harlem cafeteria

Love B. Woods & The Summit Set

Love B. Woods, the operator of the Theresa Hotel at the corner of 125th St., and Seventh Avenue, which is currently Fidel Castro's seat of Empire in the U.S., has been in the hotel business for 32 years.

The only perceptible change in his manner of walking, talking and dressing since Castro's arrival took place last Sunday, when Gamal Abdel Nasser, visited Castro at the Theresa. For that occasion, Mr. Woods bought a new light grey, snap brim hat. Immediately after Nasser's departure, Mr. Woods went back to his neat, light grey cap.

Asked if he had bought the hat especially for the occasion, Woods murmured, "I sort of needed a new hat anyway. It seemed like just as good a time as any."

Born in S. C.

Born in Columbia, S.C., "over 60 years ago," Mr. Woods attended Morris Brown College in

New York Citizen-Call (above) comments on Love B. Woods, owner of the Hotel Theresa, while (below) Woods shows new hat he bought for visit of Fidel Castro to his hotel

Outside the Hotel Theresa

(above) Fidel Castro and Juan Almeida at window of Hotel Theresa and (below) cops outside hotel

Fidel Castro with the Soviet Union's Khrushchev (above) and Egypt's Nasser (below) at the Hotel Theresa

Fidel Castro (above) at window of Hotel Theresa and (below) crowds in front of hotel

After being snubbed by President Eisenhower, Fidel Castro and Cuban delegation host a lunch for Hotel Theresa workers

The Unkindest Cut Of All

New York
Citizen-Call

15ᶜ

VOL. 1, NO. 19   Published Weekly and Copyright by the Citizen Publishing Corp., 27 West 125th St., New York 27, N. Y. Annual Subscription. $6.00; Six months. $3.50.   Application to mail at Second Class Postage Rates pending at New York, N. Y.   SATURDAY, SEPTEMBER 24, 1960   ATwater 9-7500

MR. K. & CASTRO
INVADE HARLEM
MORE TO COME!

TITO?   NASSER?   KADAR?

Front page and cartoon from *New York Citizen-Call*

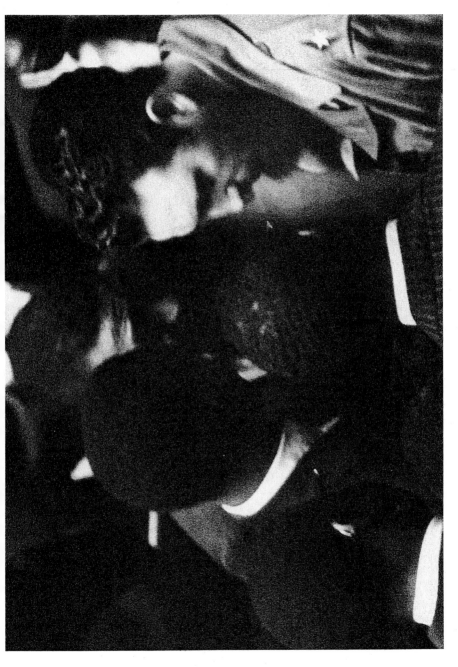

Fidel Castro with African delegates after his speech to the General
Assembly of the United Nations on September 26, 1960

Fidel Castro with delegates to the *Malcolm X Speaks in the 90s Symposium* in Havana, May 1990

His interpreter would translate longer sentences from Malcolm X into Spanish and Castro would listen alertly and smile courteously.

During their conversation, Cuba's Castro and Harlem's Malcolm covered much political and philosophical ground.

On his troubles with the Shelburne Hotel, Dr. Castro said: "They have our money — $14,000. They didn't want us to come here. When they knew we were coming here, they wanted to come along."

(He did not clarify who "they" were in this instance.)

"On racial discrimination, we work for every oppressed person." But he raised a cautioning hand. "I did not want to interfere in the inner policy of a country."

And then in a slight voice of warning, still on the general theme of racial inequity, Dr. Castro said, "I will speak in the Hall" (referring to the United Nations General Assembly).

On Africa:

"Is there any news on Lumumba?" Malcolm X smiled broadly at the mention of the Congolese leader's name. Castro then raised his hand. "We will try to defend him (Lumumba) strongly. I hope Lumumba stays here at the Theresa."

"There are 14 African nations coming to the Assembly. We are Latin Americans. We are their brothers."

On American Negroes:

Castro is fighting against discrimination in Cuba, everywhere.

"You lack rights and you want your rights."

"Our people are changing. Now we're one of the most free people in the world."

"Negroes in the U.S. have more political consciousness, more vision than anyone else."

On U.S.-Cuba relations:

In answer to Malcolm's statement that "As long as Uncle Sam is against you, you know you're a good man," Dr. Castro replied, "Not Uncle Sam. But those here who control magazines, newspapers..."

On the UN General Assembly:

"There will be a tremendous lesson to be learned at this session. Many things will happen in this session and the people will have a clearer idea of their rights."

Dr. Castro tapered the conversation off with an attempted quote of Lincoln. "You can fool some of the people some of the time..." but his English faltered and he threw up his hands as if to say, "you know what I mean."

Malcolm, rising to leave, explained his Muslim group for a Cuban reporter who had just come in. "We are followers of Muhammad. He says that we can sit and beg for 400 more years but if we want our rights now, we will have to..." Here he paused and smiled enigmatically. "Well..."

Castro smiled. He smiled again as Malcolm told him a parable. "No one knows the master better than his servants. We have been servants ever since we were brought here. We know all his little tricks. Understand? We know what he is going to do before he does."

The Cuban leader listened to this being translated into Spanish, then threw his head back and laughed heartily. "Sí," he said heartily, "Sí."

We said our adios and then walked down the crowded hall, took the elevator to the street where outside the crowds still milled around. Some excited Harlemite then shouted into the night, "Viva Castro!"

Carl Nesfield

photojournalist
Nesfield's world renowned photograph captured the historic meeting. I located him for an interview in May 1992 where he now edits his weekly paper, *The Fire and the Hammer*, from a small Harlem storefront office.

I was working as a sports editor for the *New York Citizen-Call*. I had started in the newspaper business as a photo-journalist. I would always be around shooting pictures. When I heard about Fidel coming to the Theresa, I knew that was something that I wanted to document. I went over to the Theresa and found the place surrounded by policeman from the FBI, CIA and whoever else was there. I had my police press badge on, but the cops stopped me and all of the other reporters and photographers in the lobby. You could not go up to where the Premier was. Malcolm and his entourage of two or three people came into the lobby. He was going upstairs to visit with Fidel.

For about a year of my photographic life, I was one of the photographers that Malcolm would use. He would have his people call me, and they would say, Malcolm is going to be at such and such a place, and he would like a picture, and could I make it.

I was like a freelancer. When he walked into the lobby, going up to see Fidel, seeing me he said, "Man, whatcha doing here," so I said, we were not allowed to go up. He immediately turned to the police and said, "He is with my party," so I went on upstairs with Malcolm. It was fantastic!

I was sitting on the floor, they were talking. I took a couple of shots and then some of Fidel's security people said, "OK, you will have to go now." I did not get all of the conversation, but I do remember a little thin security guy who was with Fidel. He came outside and said, "Would you like to go someplace to have a drink?" We went downstairs, and I took him across the street to the Park Cafe, which no longer exists. We had a number of drinks. That was in my drinking days. We did a lot of talking and chatting, about nothing important really. He gave me his card, I don't remember his name. I never did follow up, but he said, "Anytime you come to Cuba, look me up and everything will be at your disposal." I never went. I never spoke to him again, and I don't know where his card is at.

Being there at that moment with Malcolm and Fidel was one of the highlights of my life. To have been a part of that, to have sat there with them. I just wished that I could have stayed for all of the meeting, and to have heard all of the things they discussed.

I just took a couple of shots. I don't even think that at the time, I really realized the importance of that meeting. When you bang around the streets working in photojournalism for newspapers, I guess you get a little callous. This was just another occurrence at the time.

I haven't even had a conversation with Jimmy [Booker]. It's only been recently that I was made aware of how the picture that I took has been used over the years. I received a call from a publisher who said that he had seen my name in the newspaper under the photograph in the archives of the Schomburg.

I recently tried to get the picture copyrighted, but the copyright lawyers said that "after all of these years, you might as well forget it."

The first 10 years of my photographic career was lost. My negatives were thrown away in the trash by a landlord, including the negative of that famous picture of Fidel and Malcolm. I tried to sell the picture to a lot of the white newspapers right after the meeting, but none of them were interested. Even though none of their reporters were there, I am sure that if one of them had gotten in, they would have bought it.

The political significance of the meeting now as I see it, put Malcolm in a different light on an international basis. People here in the States may not have realized it then, but he was an important figure, known on an international level. They didn't realize how powerful his personality was. The meeting between him and Fidel showed the kinship between certain Cuban people. Not all the Cubans, not those who ran away and now control Miami. The feeling here, especially the point of view of the militants here at the time was that things had become better for the dark skinned Cubans under Castro than they had been under their predecessor Batista.

Even though I am not a traveling person, I would really like to visit Cuba.

Jimmy Booker

In reflecting back on the visit, I recall that reporters from the dailies were trying to get in the Theresa, but the police said there would be no reporters. It was a tremendous crowd. I was standing on the corner with several newspaper reporters who had come from as far away as Miami, San Francisco and Los Angeles. All of a sudden I noted a member of the African Nationalist Movement, James Rupert Lawson, who said, "Castro wants to grant an interview to some Black reporters." He then said, "Let me know who's around here." I said that I had no special reason to want to go up — being singled out when I was in this group of other reporters. So Lawson sent someone over to me and asked me to ease away over to the front of the hotel. This was between 9 and 10 o'clock in the evening. Castro and his party had been there for two to three hours. Lawson and two other militants said to come on and go with them. I remember Carl Nesfield and myself and one other reporter who was Black. The three of us went upstairs to the floor, and of course, when you got to the floor, Castro's security was very, very heavy. It was interesting that the New York police were on the main floor, and downstairs in front of the building, but on the floor where we were to meet the Premier, there were no New York policemen. If there were, they must have been in plainclothes.

The security on that floor were Castro's security men. Most of them were clad in the fatigue type uniform that they used to wear.

Castro was down on the far end of the floor overlooking 125th Street. Malcolm was on the floor already. I had talked to Malcolm downstairs. He had said that "he just wanted to welcome Fidel," along with Lawson and two or three other community activists who were on hand to give the official greeting to Harlem. That was the nature in which this meeting was framed.

Slowly they identified four or five of the militants who went in with Malcolm. I recall that we were finally ushered into the room where the Premier was plucking the chickens and then he would throw the feathers off the terrace. This was one of my first views of him [chuckle] being in Harlem. When Fidel threw the feathers off the terrace, you could hear the human cry as he went to the window.

There was a person from New York, I don't recall his name, who was serving as a sort of translator. He introduced the various people who had come to greet and to welcome the Castro party to Harlem. The translator introduced Malcolm and Malcolm nodded and bowed to Mr. Castro. They exchanged pleasantries and discussed points about the struggle.

It was not a heavy conversation, lasting approximately 15 minutes, and between the interpreter and comments from one to the other along with comments made by other persons, it wasn't really a hard news story. It was an exchange of pleasantries — a greeting in terms of the struggle, briefly expressing what it meant to each one of them.

For me, there was no hard meat, in terms of substance for a story. I wrote a story, but there weren't enough strong quotes in it for me to really get a hard nuts and bolts story. It just was not there in the content of the meeting.

[Booker acknowledged, that inspite of having an interpreter in the meeting, the language barrier was a factor which limited his ability to converse.]

Oddly enough at the end, I had four to five papers coming to me after the meeting, wanting to know what was said. And I said, look, I work for the *Amsterdam News* and I wasn't giving anybody any quotes. The papers did mention that there had been a meeting. My deadline had been the day before. I had to wait a whole week before my article came out.

I would not give any comments and quotes to anybody there because I felt that my first obligation was to my own newspaper.

The day before Malcolm was murdered, I ran into him and

Muhammad Ali. I invited them up to my apartment for tea and we talked. During the discussion, they both brought up the meeting between him and Fidel in the Hotel Theresa.

I don't remember any of the content of the conversation between Malcolm and Fidel, except that Malcolm told Fidel, "It was so good of you to come to our community." I recall that Malcolm also expressed that it was good to see [Fidel] continue his struggle for all Black people, and he used all of the other various racial phrases in terms of his supporting the Black causes, in terms of the international struggle that he was conducting.

Not being a scholar, I saw it as a meeting of two people. In the eyes of the press and as a reporter, and not as an editorial thinker, the meeting of the two was not played up as a significant encounter. I remember it as a fleeting moment.

Reinaldo Peñalver
Cuban journalist

The presence of Comrade Fidel and the Cuban delegation in Harlem became something of an event. Not only the hotel, but the entire neighborhood was considered the host. There was a popular mobilization, 24-hours a day. Everytime Fidel left for the United Nations or came back, there was always a demonstration, chanting "Long live Castro!" Hundreds of men and women were always cheering Fidel.

For those who lived in Harlem the police were always surrounding the hotel, sort of an affront to the dignity of the neighborhood. Some of the leaders among them said that Fidel did not need more protection than "the people of Harlem." The Black Muslims offered to take care of the security of Fidel and they were demanding that the police be retired. Fidel agreed to this in principle, but Fidel's security team convinced the people of Harlem that this measure could bring about a confrontation with the Cuban reactionaries belonging to the group La Rosa Blanca. This group was looking for every opportunity to create an "incident" outside the hotel.

New York Citizen-Call
September 24, 1960
A New Kind of Crowd

Some 2,000 brown New Yorkers stood in the rain Monday night

waiting for Cuba's Premier Fidel Castro to arrive at Harlem's famous old Hotel Theresa.

There was little of the usual Harlem cynicism. Perhaps as the first people gathered someone might have said, "Now you know Castro isn't coming up here among all us Negroes."

A sentiment like that might have been passed along at the beginning. But as the crowd grew larger, as the dark night sky began to yield to more and more raised umbrellas, the mood of the people grew rigid.

In short time, no one questioned that Fidel Castro would not come to Harlem to spend his remaining time in this country.

The crowd's mood hardened. Fidel Castro would arrive. The only question now was, "what time?"

People pressed forward against the police barricades as if by drawing closer to the hotel's entrance, that action alone would speed the bearded Premier's arrival.

The thoughtful observer sensed that these people wanted Castro to come to Harlem.

And from the conversations among this rain soaked mass of humanity, the idea began to build that Castro would come here to stay because he had found out, as most Negroes found out, the nasty ways the underdog was treated downtown.

To Harlem's oppressed ghetto dwellers, Castro was that bearded revolutionary who had thrown the nation's rascals out and who had told white America to go to hell.

Fair Play for Cuba Committee

Journalist Bob Taber had been a main player in organizing the Fair Play for Cuba Committee. He frequented Cuba during the early days of the guerrilla movement. His book *M-26 — The Biography of a Revolution*, details the rise of the July 26 Movement led by the young lawyer Fidel Castro and his tiny force of Cuban patriots who launched the July 1953 assault on the Moncada Barracks in Santiago de Cuba. The military garrison was a stronghold of the Batista dictatorship.

According to Fair Play for Cuba Committee documents, the organization was "formed to help set the record straight, to expose the lies of those who want to get back into Cuba for lost profits from investments and politics. To get back could mean nuclear war. We must protest and continue to protest; we must shout at the top of our lungs to prevent any military intervention in Cuba. We must make known the consequences of any continuation, no less the accentuation of present U.S. policy. To keep up this cry of 'Hands off Cuba'."

The Fair Play for Cuba Committee was a national organization, launched in April 1960, with chapters throughout much of the United States, spilling into Canada. The organization was a significant force in challenging the distortions and misinformation propagated by the mainstream media to the U.S. public.

The Committee successfully mobilized support for Fidel Castro and the Cuban delegation upon their arrival in New York to participate in the UN General Assembly. In addition, the New York chapter of the Fair Play for Cuba Committee held a reception for the delegation in the Hotel Theresa banquet hall on September 21. Hosted by African American Richard Gibson, president of the Committee, among those attending were poet Langston Hughes, C. Wright Mills, Allen Ginsberg and French photographer Henri Cartier-Bresson.

Fidel in Harlem
October 7, 1960 Fair Play for Cuba Committee newsletter

Even the New York tabloids failed to disguise the magnificent welcome that the Prime Minister and his delegation received in Harlem. The reception given by the New York chapter, FPCC, attended by some 200 members (apologies to others whom we were unable to contact in time) was only part of it. Fidel, accepting a bust of Lincoln from Chapter President Richard Gibson on behalf of the national committee ("From one liberator to another," ad libbed Gibson), said that he felt like a man traveling through a desert who suddenly reached an oasis.

Outside the venerable Hotel Theresa, a Harlem crowd that ranged upward in number from several hundred to several thousands, depending on the time of day or night, kept a round-the-clock watch for occasional glimpses of the famous visitor, and voiced a boisterous goodwill that was the exact opposite of what the visiting Cubans had encountered during their brief stay in the fashionable midtown hotel.

Reinaldo Peñalver

The historic context of the meeting was between the redeemer and with those still to be redeemed. Leaders such as Richard Gibson who gave Fidel a bust of Abraham Lincoln said when he presented it, "from one liberator to another liberator." This meeting took place in the main hall of the Theresa Hotel. Among those that I remember being there was the writer Carleton Beals [*The Crime of Cuba*]. Fidel greatly appreciated the moment and said, "I feel like a person who has been walking through the desert who suddenly feels that he has found an oasis. We know," Fidel said, "what propaganda can do, but we also know that in spite of the propaganda, we have many friends in the United States. For that we are stronger, and the stronger the propaganda, the stronger we become."

At the same time, Fidel gave the the owner of the hotel, Mr. Love, a bust of José Martí that had the dedication: "It is a sin against humanity to promote oppression and hatred among races."

There was also an unexpected meeting at the hotel, even though Fidel tried not to make public appearances. [The Cubans had taken this position as a measure to prevent the U.S. government from accusing them of public disturbances.] Once he had to greet the people that were cheering on the street. He went out on the balcony and thousands of Cuban flags were waved and he was rousingly cheered. At that moment, around 127th St., a great crowd appeared of Latin Americans from Puerto Rico, the Dominican Republic and Mexico. They had organized a demonstration down Broadway and then into the street in front of the hotel. There was a real integration of the races, dominated by the revolutionary fever of those present. They were cheering "Cuba sí! Yankee no! Patria or muerte! [Land or death]" and all the Blacks from Harlem were chanting, "We want Castro, we want Fidel!"

Booker Johnson
Former associate of Malcolm X and member of the Nation of Islam. Chef at Muhammad Ali Training Camp.
Booker Johnson remembered that he and several other Muslim brothers, including former heavyweight boxing champion Joe Louis, had just received their charter for an export-import business the same day Fidel arrived at the Hotel Theresa.

Some Cuban friends had already spoken to Fidel about the possibilities of our Black company trading with the new revolutionary government. I did not know it then, but Castro's main man and I were personal friends. The one they caught with the boat with the guns in it going to Cuba from Florida, that was my personal friend. We use to drink coffee and talk politics, and then when Castro came to Harlem, I saw him and someone else who was close to another friend of mine with Castro. We were all set aback! Here was someone that we drank coffee with and talked to about nationalism and Islam and everything, and then it turns out that some of his main operatives were in Harlem. They lived in Harlem right here with us!

Brother Louis X even went to Cuba to make arrangements for doing business, but by that time, the U.S. government had slapped the embargo against them, and trading was limited to medicines, and we weren't doing any business in that area. [Within a few years, the embargo was to prohibit even the sale of medicines and food to Cuba.]

Conrad Lynn
Attorney Lynn had visited Cuba some months prior to Fidel's arrival in the U.S.

We Blacks and revolutionaries said then that we would force the revolution in the United States if the government attacked Fidel. And I still say that today.

Well, when he came up, it was raining that day. That didn't make any difference to the Black people in Harlem. They were there by the thousand. They surrounded that hotel by the thousands, as far as I could see. They had their umbrellas and when he came out on the balcony, there was a wrought iron balcony, they were just screaming, "Fidel! Fidel!" He was their man!

I also remember that we were together in the hotel with Fidel, along with his Chief of Staff of the Army, who was a Black man. I can't remember his name. [Major Juan Almeida Bosque]

During his stay, Fidel made a tour of Harlem, and the people followed him by the hundreds of thousands. They don't want to talk about that; even today, they are a little slow to talk about that great homage that was paid to Fidel Castro by the people of Harlem.

Lynn said that an intermediary put Fidel in touch with him when he arrived in the United States. Lynn also told me that he and Fidel talked about the future prospects for Black revolutionaries in the United States.

I was not that young at the time. I was more mature about a lot of things. I told Fidel that I did not feel that a revolutionary period was imminent in the United States. However, on the question of an attack by the United States against Cuba, I told him that we could arouse a real revolutionary movement in this country, because the Black people, even if they were not communist, they — like the Black communist — still liked the freedom which Cuba had attained and they admired Fidel Castro.

As a whole, even the conservative Black people that I knew admired Fidel Castro.

For example the manifesto that we put out which was signed by Robert Williams, myself and others [See Cuba, a Declaration of Conscience by Afro Americans *signed by 27 African Americans*] was a matter of propaganda to a large degree. We weren't so unrealistic as to really think that we could stir up revolution in the United States if the United States attacked Cuba.

Our declaration was a propaganda position at that time, and I still raise that possibility today — that the people always have the option, the right of revolution. Fidel is the living embodiment of that position. That is why they have always tried to get rid of Fidel, to kill him. Because he is still there — because Fidel still survives — it means that revolution remains an option for the American people.

The visit of Fidel to Harlem symbolized the possibilities of Black people being in the leadership of a revolutionary movement in the United States.

Booker Johnson
The people stayed in the street all night. Fidel had a look-alike, and about every half hour, he would come to the window and wave a towel, and that went on until the next morning. It was a psychological thing. That's right, 'bout every half hour, this brother who looked like Castro would come to the window, wave the white towel, and the people would just begin to holler. His commander, a little man, would come and sit in Chock Full O'Nuts and drink coffee with us. That's how real they were.

Reinaldo Peñalver
When Juan Almeida arrived at the hotel on September 21, 1960, after walking through several blocks of the neighborhood, he

immediately became a popular figure and from then on wherever he went, he was followed by an enormous multitude of people cheering him on.

Love B. Woods, the proprietor of the Hotel Theresa at the time of Fidel's visit, has been immortalized by almost everyone who knew him. Almost everyone that I interviewed spoke of the respect Love garnered when he refused to back down in his commitment to host the Cuban delegation.

At the time of Fidel's visit, some say Love was well into his late 80s. He was a vocal and respected leader in the Harlem community. Having acquired the Theresa only four months before the controversial guest arrived, Love held his ground against a barrage of red baiting and anti-Cuba hysteria. Confronted not only by groups such as La Rosa Blanca, there were also rumblings from the quarters of "Negro" ministers and the popular Harlem leader, Adam Clayton Powell, Jr.

Powell along with some of the ministerial groups issued scathing denunciations to the press of the Cuban leader's visit to Harlem, calling it a "publicity stunt."

Powell, Democrat leader and House of Representatives member, was vehemently opposed to Fidel staying at the Theresa. A statement released to the *New York Times* quoted him: "We Negro people have enough problems of our own without the additional burden of Dr. Castro's confusion."

The *Amsterdam News*, one of the major Black weeklies, reported the comments from an address delivered by Gloster B. Current, national director of NAACP branches to the North Carolina State Conference of NAACP Branches: "Negroes are not fooled by the communist... They are attempting to call attention to the plight of Negroes in northern communities where housing is at a premium. That is why we continue to point out to Americans that the denying of civil rights in our nation, and especially in the south, harms our nation abroad. Two-thirds of the world is colored."

Nonetheless, the opposition that did exist, did not phase the people of Harlem. Bill Epton has pointed out in his essay that "the reality of Harlem's residents had already seasoned them in the throes of the political struggle against the tyranny of police, landlords and Jim Crow racism."

Fidel Castro's stay in Harlem was transformed by the community into another form of resistance against the state. The daily outpouring into the Harlem streets reflected the independent thinking of a people who knew only too well what it felt like to be treated as second class and disenfranchised. It is no wonder that

Love B. Woods held his ground.

The Cuban delegation was also excluded from a luncheon hosted by President Eisenhower for heads of Latin American delegations to the General Assembly. Upon returning to his hotel, Fidel hosted a luncheon at the Theresa, where he invited all of the employees. Not only did the workers respond positively, but Love Woods even made it his business to personally attend and commented on the manner in which the Cubans were being treated by the U.S. government.

Reinaldo Peñalver

Mr. Woods said in an interview that he "didn't believe, and didn't even care if there might be reprisals against [him] or against the neighbors of Harlem." Because as he said, "We have had the honor of receiving Fidel Castro in our home and receiving him as he deserves. With or without Castro, we have been suffering reprisals and repression since the day that we were born. I know, because I have lived it." He also commented on what he termed "the maneuvers that some people have carried out to show their lack of courtesy. First of all it was the confinement [of Fidel] to Manhattan, and then secondly, it was the high guarantee that [Fidel] had to make in order to be lodged in a hotel. That is why I decided to open my hotel to receive Commander Fidel Castro, and I am very happy because I have a gentlemen in my home."

Booker Johnson

Fidel gave Love B. Woods $40,000. Love B. Woods lost that hotel and done 30 days in jail 'cause he wouldn't tell them [the Federal Government] what he done with the money. Love B. Woods was a personal friend of mine. He told me that right after he got out of jail. Unfortunately, he got hit by a car and didn't live very long afterwards. Basically that money was his nephew's money who didn't have any education. Mr. Woods and his brother, who was the treasurer and the brain behind the business, were the ones who controlled the money. It's on record where he wouldn't tell the U.S. government what he did with the money, because they wanted to tax it. Woods would not tell them what he did with it, and they gave him 30 days in jail!

Walie Muhammad

Former associate of Malcolm X and member of the Nation of Islam. Trainer of Muhammad Ali, friend and associate of Booker Johnson.

It was amazing and history in the making to have seen so many great leaders visiting Harlem when Castro was here. We were happy to see him come up to Harlem, and happy to see so many of his followers in North America stand by him. We were glad to see that togetherness. Castro was speaking Black and we were Black people, and we were interested in anyone trying to bring the Black peoples together throughout the planet earth.

Raúl Roa Kouri

Malcolm X was not confused whatsoever with the projections of the Cuban revolution. He was not confused about Fidel's projection. The political thinking of Malcolm in 1960 was developing. His concepts were much narrower, but what is interesting to note is that, as years went on, the political thinking of Malcolm became much more profound, much more revolutionary, encompassing all of U.S. society. I think that this is very important, and I would say that the cardinal importance of his talks with Fidel was precisely this, of his understanding that the poor were not only Blacks, even though they were the more oppressed, that they had been terribly discriminated against, but that there were other brothers, other comrades who are equally humiliated and oppressed in that society. The Indians, the Chicanos, the Hispanics were also repressed by U.S. society and the struggle of all was a common struggle.

I would say that this was one of the topics analyzed by Fidel and Malcolm X. I also believe that this was the final route of the political thought of Malcolm X and that was precisely why he was assassinated... The importance of Malcolm X and his ideas are still valid for all of the oppressed in the United States today... The meeting between Malcolm and Fidel back in 1960 was undoubtedly a fruitful stimulus for Malcolm X's thinking and for our own knowledge of the true situation of the oppressed in the United States. I think that it is very important today, more than ever, for the followers of Malcolm X in the United States and the Cuban revolutionaries to act together.

Reinaldo Peñalver

[My having the opportunity to meet with Malcolm X was] not a coincidence, it was something that I had envisaged in Havana... from the moment that I found out that I was to be a member of the delegation traveling to the United Nations.

In 1959, at the beginning of the revolution, a program was convened titled "Operation Truth." It brought to Cuba journalists from the United States, most of them Black journalists, representing the magazine *Ebony* and other Black publications such as the *Chicago Defender*.

Many journalists came to see what was going to happen to their Black brothers following the triumph of the revolution. The Batista dictatorship had disseminated propaganda saying, "Fidel was a racist and that in the Sierra Maestra [mountains] there were no Blacks fighting." They also said that when Fidel had triumphed, he would "exterminate all Blacks." Of course this was done to try to prevent Blacks from supporting Fidel's movement. This wasn't done overtly, but covertly. There were rumors which just spread. For example, I remember that at some parties there would be a lot of Blacks, and then some leaflets would appear that said "you Blacks better heat up your feet dancing, because Fidel's gonna really cool your heels."

There were also, among those [U.S.] journalists, some who wanted to know more of the problems the revolution was confronting. This is when I met Everett Muhammad, who was representing the paper *Muhammad Speaks*. He spoke with a lot of emphasis about Malcolm X and about Malcolm's ideas, his life and actions.

Everett told me that Malcolm was a fabulous person. I was very interested in what he had to say about him, so as soon as I reached New York, one of my main objectives was to make contact with Malcolm X and have an interview with him.

From the very first, I was particularly impressed by his personality, by his intelligence, and by the way that he was speaking. From the very beginning of the interview, we were able to establish great communication. So great, that instead of me interviewing him, he interviewed me. Malcolm already knew who Fidel was, he already knew the objectives of the revolution because Everett Muhammad had already told him. I remember very well the conversation that I had with Malcolm. It was fraternal and brotherly. He asked me about discrimination in Cuba, how Blacks lived in Cuba and the future role of Blacks within the revolution. Among other things, he wanted to know what were the possibilities of establishing a branch of the Black Muslims in Cuba. I said that I did not think that it was possible because the conditions in Cuba were not the same as they were in the United States. What we had suffered in Cuba before the triumph of the revolution was not the same as that which Blacks had suffered in the United States. Malcolm was astonished at the sense of our togetherness — by the fact that there were Black and white officials who were a part of the delegation.

We laughed together and he said, "I came here to be interviewed, and I am the one who is interviewing you."

Malcolm at one point said, "I am very interested in Cuba and also because the only white person that I have really liked was Fidel." He then said, "the rest of them for me are devils." And I asked, "But what about the other comrades?" and he said, "They are devils too! Except for Fidel, all the rest are devils." It was something, mostly very funny. Malcolm laughed and said, "You Cubans have a very advanced sense of humor."

Malcolm told me that he would visit Cuba, but at that moment he was very busy. He was involved with his work in the Black Muslims which meant he travelled to a lot of cities. But he promised me that as soon as he could, he would visit Cuba. "To be able to see for myself, everything that you have told me," he said.

We are very sorry that he was never able to visit Cuba.

Malcolm X

Malcolm may never have had the chance to visit Cuba, but in his autobiography he left this observation of Fidel's visit to Harlem:

The Theresa is now best known as the place where Fidel Castro went during his UN visit, and achieved *a psychological coup over the U.S. State Department* [emphasis added] when it confined him to Manhattan, never dreaming that he'd stay uptown in Harlem and make such an impression among the Negroes.

These observations were reinforced on December 13, 1964 when Malcolm made these comments on a proposed visit to Harlem by Che Guevara.

I have the greatest honor to introduce the minister of cooperatives and commerce from Tanzania, Sheik Abdul Rahman Muhammad Babu. He's just left a dinner with another very good friend of ours, and I say a very good friend of ours. I want to point this out to you, I don't let anybody choose my friends. And you shouldn't let anybody choose your friends. You and I should practice the habit of weighing peoples and weighing situations and weighing groups and weighing governments for ourselves. And don't let somebody else tell us who our enemies should be and who our friends should be.

I love a revolutionary. And one of the most revolutionary men in this country right now was going to come out here along with our friend, Sheik Babu, but he thought better of it. But he did send this message. It says:

Dear brothers and sisters of Harlem,

I would have liked to have been with you and Brother Babu, but the actual conditions are not good for this meeting. Receive the warm salutations of the Cuban people and especially those of Fidel, who remembers enthusiastically his visit to Harlem a few years ago. United we will win.

This is from Che Guevara. I am happy to hear your warm round of applause in return, because it lets the man know that he's just not in a position today to tell us who we should applaud for and who we shouldn't applaud for. And you don't see any anti-Castro Cubans around here — we eat them up.

Let them go and fight the Ku Klux Klan, or the White Citizens Council. Let them spend some of that energy getting their own house in order. Don't come up to Harlem and tell us who we should applaud for and shouldn't applaud for. Or there will be some ex-anti-Castro Cubans.

Fidel Castro
At the conclusion of the *Malcolm X Speaks in the 90s Symposium* in Havana on May 24, 1990, Fidel Castro made the following observations on his 1960 visit to Harlem.

We have always been in solidarity with the struggle of Black people, of minorities, and of the poor in the United States. We have always been in solidarity with them, and they have been in solidarity with us.

We must fight to defeat the campaigns, the schemes, and the lies, all that is aimed at separating us. I think that in these times we need that friendship more than ever, and we need your solidarity more than ever. And we fully appreciate it, because we understand that one has to be very courageous to organize a rally supporting Cuba in the United States.

The value of the action cannot be measured by the number of people participating, but by the fact that they participate, by the courage it took to do so in moments when socialism seemed to be collapsing.

And it is really collapsing in many countries where there never was true socialism. One of the premises of true socialism is that it arise from the people themselves. It cannot be given or built for you; it has to spring from the struggle of the people itself, as has been the case of socialism in Cuba.

In spite of those disasters, we feel more committed than ever to socialism and to the revolution, to defending it and proving that it is a thousand times superior to any other social system. I think this is in the interest of all the peoples.

If reactionary ideas prevail, if they gain supremacy in the world, that supremacy will be directed against all the Third World countries. Those reactionary forces will direct their supremacy against the people of the United States itself. This is a fact, because those who attack us are also the enemies of all just causes everywhere in the world, including in the United States.

Cuba has an important role to play, a very big responsibility, because there were people who thought that the revolution here would collapse just like socialism fell over there. They had set the date, day and month. There were people in Miami already packing their bags to come over here. Their clothes will be eaten by moths!

But of course, this country will resist. We are waging three great battles: the political battle, where we maintain the unity of the people, the support of the people, the determination of our people; the economic battle, which is even more difficult here than elsewhere given the conditions we face; and the battle for defense.

We have to work in these three directions. But we are not doing this for ourselves. We are doing it for all the just causes of the world, at a time of skepticism. Optimism and the hope of the peoples will again be born, because the negative forces will not prevail.

We want the people of the United States — Black people, Latinos, Asians, and all the nationalities within the United States, everyone with a spirit of justice — to understand this.

We are very grateful that you have participated in this meeting in Cuba, in this seminar in remembrance of Malcolm X. Now, more than ever, we have to remember Malcolm X, Che [Guevara], and all the heroes of the struggle and the cause of the peoples. That is why the importance and significance you give to this anniversary has gladdened me so much.

I always recall my meeting with Malcolm X at the Hotel Theresa, because he was the one who supported us and made it possible for us to stay there. We faced two alternatives. One was the United Nations gardens — when I mentioned this to the Secretary-General, he was horrified at the thought of a delegation in tents there. But when we received Malcom X's offer — he had spoken with one of our comrades — I said, "That is the place, the Hotel Theresa." And there we went. So I have a personal recollection very much linked to him.

Years passed and I regret not having had more time to speak with him, because those days in New York were rough. It was madness. There were quite a number of people who had already left for the United States, a large number of Cubans who were against the revolution, and there were others who had resided there for a long time who were in favor. And then there were many people from the United States giving us "thumbs down" in the streets. But when we arrived in Harlem it was the complete opposite.

Almeida was with us; we were a little younger then. In fact, we didn't know much about politics. But we had a rebel spirit, a spirit of struggle. We were convinced of our cause. Of course, we did not have the experience that we inevitably have accumulated over many years. But we are still here, and we intend to continue being the cause of headaches.

Cuba Libre

by LeRoi Jones (Amiri Baraka)

Amiri Baraka's (LeRoi Jones) award winning essay *Cuba Libre* is an important contribution to this volume. The renowned writer-activist's words were a chilling reminder then as they are a warning now — that we must reject "the cold light of 'reason'." That 'reason,' Baraka wrote, "being whatever repugnant lie our usurious 'ruling class' had paid their journalists to disseminate."

In July 1960, along with a group of other African Americans, Baraka, who was editor of Yugen magazine, went to Cuba on a trip arranged by the Fair Play for Cuba Committee. While there, he went to the Sierra Maestra mountains in Oriente province to attend a mass anniversary rally of the Cuban revolution. *Cuba Libre* records his impressions of that historic journey.

It was late at night, and still Havana had not settled down to its usual quiet. Crowds of people were squatting around bus stops, walking down the streets in groups headed for bus stops. Truckloads of militia were headed out of the city. Young men and women with rucksacks and canteens were piling into buses, trucks, and private cars all over the city. There were huge signs all over Havana reading "A La Sierra Con Fidel... Julio 26." Thousands of people were leaving Havana for the July 26 celebration in the Sierra Maestra all the way at the other end of the island in Oriente province. The celebration was in honor of Fidel Castro's first onslaught against Moncada barracks July 26, 1953, which marked the beginning of his drive against the Batista government. Whole families were packing up, trying to get to Oriente the best way they could. It was still three days before the celebration and people clogged the roads from Havana all the way to the eastern province.

The night of our departure for Oriente we arrived at the train station in Havana about six p.m. It was almost impossible to move around in the station. *Campesinos* (peasant farmers), businessmen, soldiers, *milicianas*, tourists — all were thrashing around trying to make sure they had seats in the various trains. As we came into the station, most of the delegates of a Latin American Youth Congress were coming in also. There were about 900 of them, representing students from almost every country in Latin America. Mexicans, Colombians, Argentines, Venezuelans, Puerto Ricans (with signs reading, "For the Liberation of Puerto Rico"), all carrying flags, banners, and wearing the large, ragged straw hat of the *campesino*. We were to go in the same train as the delegates.

As we moved through the crowds towards our train, the students began chanting: "Cuba sí, Yanqui no... Cuba sí, Yanqui no... Cuba sí, Yanqui no." The crowds in the terminal joined in; soon there was a deafening crazy scream that seemed to burst the roof off the terminal. Cuba sí, Yanqui no! We raced for the trains.

Once inside the train, a long, modern semi-air-conditioned "Silver Meteor," we quickly settled down and I began scribbling illegibly in my notebook. But the Latin Americans came scrambling into the train still chanting furiously and someone handed me a drink of rum. They were yelling "Venceremos, Venceremos, Venceremos, Venceremos" ("We will win"). Crowds of soldiers and militia on the platform outside joined in. Everyone was screaming as the train began to pull away.

The young militia people soon came trotting through the coaches asking everyone to sit down for a few seconds so they could be counted. The delegates got to their seats and in my coach everyone began to sing a song like "two, four, six, eight, who do we appreciate... Fidel, Fidel, Fidel!!" Then they did Che (Guevara), Raúl, President Dorticos, etc. It was about 1,000 kilometers to Oriente and we had just started.

Young soldiers passed out ham sandwiches and Maltina, a thick syrupy sweet beverage that only made me thirstier. Everyone in the train seemed to be talking excitedly and having a wild time. We were about an hour outside Havana and I was alternating between taking notes and reading about ancient Mexican religion when Olga Finlay, our interpreter, came up to my seat accompanied by a young woman. "I told her you were an American poet," Olga said, "and she wanted to meet you." I rose quickly and extended my hand, for some reason embarrassed as hell. Olga said, "Senora Betancourt, Senor LeRoi Jones." She was very short, very blonde and very pretty, and had a weird accent that never ceased to fascinate me. For about 30 minutes we stood in the middle aisle talking to each other. She was a Mexican delegate to the Youth Congress, a graduate student in economics at one of the universities, the wife of an economist, and a mother. Finally, I offered her the seat next to mine at the window. She sat, and we talked almost continuously throughout the 14-hour ride.

She questioned me endlessly about American life, American politics, American youth — although I was jokingly cautioned against using the word American to mean the United States or North America. "Everyone in this car is American," she said. "You from the North, we from the South." I explained as best I could about the Eisenhowers, the Nixons, the DuPonts, but she made even my condemnations seem mild. "Everyone in the world," she said, with her finger, has to be communist or anti-communist. And if they're anti-communist, no matter what kind of foul person they are, you people accept them as your allies. Do you really think that hopeless little island in the middle of the sea is China? That is irrational. You people are irrational!"

I tried to defend myself, "Look, why jump on me? I understand what you're saying. I'm in complete agreement with you. I'm a poet... what can I do? I write, that's all, I'm not even interested in politics."

She jumped on me with both feet as did a group of Mexican poets later in Havana. She called me a "cowardly bourgeois individual..." The poets, or at least one young, wild eyed Mexican poet, Jaime Shelley, almost left me in tears, stomping his foot on the floor, screaming: "You want to cultivate your soul? In that ugliness you live in, you want to cultivate your soul? Well, we've got millions of starving people to feed, and that moves me enough to make poems out of."

Around 10 p.m. the train pulled into the town of Matanzas. We had our blinds drawn, but the militia came running through the car telling us to raise them. When I raised the blind I was almost startled out of my wits. There were about 1,500 people in the train station and surrounding it, yelling their lungs out. We pulled up the windows. People were all over. They ran back and forth along the train screaming at us. The Mexicans in the train had a big sign painted on a bedspread that read "Mexico is with Fidel. Venceremos." When they raised it to the windows young men leaped in the air, and women blew kisses. There was a uniformed marching band trying to be heard above the crowd, but I could barely hear them. When I poked my head out of the window to wave at the crowds, two young Negro women giggled violently at first, then one of them ran over to the train and kissed me as hard as she could manage. The only thing to do I could think of was to say, "Thank you." She danced up and down and clapped her hands and shouted to her friend, "Un americano, un americano." I bowed my head graciously.

What was it, a circus? That wild, mad crowd. Social ideas? Could there be that much excitement generated through all the people? Damn, that people still *can* move. Not us, but people. It's gone out of us forever. "Cuba sí, Yanqui no." I called at the girls as the train edged away.

We stopped later in the town of Colon. There again, the same mobs of cheering people. Camaguey, Santa Clara. At each town, the chanting crowds. The unbelievable joy and excitement. The same idea, and people made beautiful because of it. People moving, being moved, I was ecstatic and frightened. Something I had never seen before, exploding all around me.

The train rocked wildly across and into the interior. The delegates were singing a "cha cha" with words changed to something like "Fidel, Fidel, cha cha cha, Che Che, cha cha cha, abajo imperialismo yanqui, cha cha cha." Some American students whom I hadn't seen earlier ran back and forth in the coaches singing "We cannot be moved." The young folk-song politicians in blue jeans and pigtails.

About two o'clock in the morning they shut the lights off in most of the coaches, and everybody went to sleep. I slept for only an hour or so and woke up just in time to see the red sun come up and the first, early people come out of their small grass-roofed shacks beside the railroad tracks, and wave sleepily at the speeding train. I pressed my face against the window and waved back.

The folk singing and war cries had just begun again in earnest when we reached the town of Yara, a small town in Oriente province, the last stop on the line. At once we unloaded from the train, leaving most luggage and whatever was considered superfluous. The dirt streets of the town were jammed with people. Probably everyone in town had come to meet the train. The entire town was decorated with some kind of silver Christmas tree tinsel and streamers. Trees, bushes, houses, children, all draped in the same silver holiday tinsel. Tiny girls in brown uniforms and red berets greeted us with armfuls of flowers. Photographers were running amok through the crowd, including an American newsreel cameraman who kept following Robert Williams, a member of our group. I told Robert that he ought to put his big straw hat in front of his face, American gangster style.

From the high hill of the train station it was possible to see a road running right through Yara. Every conceivable kind of bus, truck, car and scooter was being pushed toward the Sierra, which was now plainly visible in the distance. Some of the *campesinos* were on horses, dodging in and out of the sluggish traffic, screaming at the top of their lungs.

The sun had already gotten straight up over our heads and was burning down viciously. The big straw *campesino* hats helped a little but I could tell that it was going to be an obscenely hot day. We stood around for a while until everyone had gotten off our train, and then some of the militia people waved at us to follow them. We walked completely out of the town of Yara in about two minutes. We walked until we came to more railroad tracks; a short spur leading off in the direction of Sierra Maestra. Sitting on the tracks were about 10 empty open cattle cars. There were audible groans from the American contingent. The cars themselves looked like movable jails. Huge thick bars around the sides. We joked about the American cameraman taking a picture of them with us behind the bars and using it as a *Life* magazine cover. They would caption it "Americans in Cuba."

At a word from the militia we scrambled up through the bars, into the scalding cars. The metal parts of the car were burning hot, probably from sitting out in the sun all day. It was weird seeing hundreds of people up and down the tracks climbing up into the cattle cars by whatever method they could manage. We had been told in Havana that this was going to be a rough trip and that we ought to dress accordingly. Heavy shoes, old clothes, a minimum of equipment. The women were told specifically to wear slacks and flat shoes because it would be difficult to walk up a mountain in a sheath dress and heels. However, one of the American women, a pretty, young middle-class lady from Philadelphia, showed up in a flare skirt and "Cuban" heels. Two of the Cubans had to pull and tug to get her into the car, which still definitely had the smell of cows. She slumped in a corner and began furiously mopping her brow.

I sat down on the floor and tried to scribble in my notebook, but it was difficult because everyone was jammed in very tight. Finally, the train jerked to a start, and everyone in all the cars let out a wild yell. The delegates began chanting again. Waving at all the people along the road, and all the dark, barefoot families standing in front of their grass-topped huts calling to us. The road which ran along parallel to the train was packed full of traffic, barely moving. Men sat on the running boards of their cars when the traffic came to a complete halt, and drank water from their canteens. The train was going about five miles an hour and the *campesinos* raced by on their plow horses jeering, swinging their big hats. The sun and the hot metal car were almost unbearable. The delegates shouted at the trucks, "Cuba sí, Yanqui no," and then began their "Viva" shouts. After one of the "Vivas," I yelled "Viva Calle Cuaranta y dos" (42nd St.), "Viva Symphony Sid," "Viva Cinco Punto" (Five Spot), "Viva Turban Boy." I guess it was the heat. It was a long, slow ride in the boiling cars.

The cattle cars stopped after an hour or so at some kind of junction. All kinds of other coaches were pulled up and resting on various spurs. People milled about everywhere. But it was the end of any tracks going further towards Sierra. We stood around and drank warm water too fast.

Now we got into trucks. Some with nailed in bus seats, some with straw roofs, others with just plain truck floors. It was a wild scramble for seats. The militia people and the soldiers did their best to indicate which trucks were for whom, but people staggered into the closest vehicle at hand. Ed Clarke, the young Negro abstract expressionist painter, and I ran and leaped up into a truck with leather bus seats in the back. The leather was too hot to sit on for a while so I put my handkerchief on the seat and sat lightly. A woman was trying to get up into the truck, but not very successfully, so I leaned over the rail and pulled her up and in. The face was recognizable immediately, but I had to sit back on the hot seat before I remembered it was Francoise Sagan. I turned to say something to her, but some men were already helping her back down to the ground. She rode up front in the truck's cab with a young lady companion, and her manager on the running board, clinging to the door.

The trucks reared out onto the already heavily traveled road. It was an unbelievable scene. Not only all the weird trucks and buses but thousands of people walking along the road. Some had walked from places as far away as Matanzas. Whole detachments of militia were marching, rout step, but carrying rifles or 45's. Women carrying children on their shoulders. One group of militia with blue shirts, green pants, pistols and knives, was carrying paper fans, which they ripped back and forth almost in unison with their step. There were huge trucks full of oranges parked along the road with lines of people circling them. People were sitting along the edge of the road eating their lunches. Everyone going "a la Sierra."

Our trucks sped along on the outside of the main body of traffic, still having to stop occasionally when there was some hopeless roadblock. The sun, for all our hats, was baking our heads. Sweat poured in my dry mouth. None of us Americans had brought canteens and there was no water to be had while we were racing along the road. I tried several times to get some oranges, but never managed. The truck would always start up again when we came close to an orange vendor.

There was a sign on one of the wood shack "stores" we passed that read "Ninos No Gustan Los Chicles Ni Los Cigarros Americanos Ni El Rocan Rool." It was signed "Fondin." The traffic bogged down right in front of the store so several French photographers leaped off the truck and raced for the orange stand. Only one fellow managed to make it back to our truck with a hat full of oranges. The others had to turn and run back empty handed as the truck pulled away. Sagan's manager, who had strapped himself on the running board with a leather belt, almost broke his head when the truck hit a bump and the belt snapped and sent him sprawling into the road. Another one of the correspondents suddenly became violently ill and tried to shove his head between the rough wooden slats at the side of the truck; he didn't quite make it, and everyone in the truck suffered.

After two hours we reached a wide, slow, muddy river. There was only one narrow cement bridge crossing it, so the trucks had to wait until they could ease back into the regular line of traffic. There were hundreds of people wading across the river. A woman splashed in with her child on her shoulders, hanging around her neck, her lunch pail in one hand, a pair of blue canvas sneakers in the other. One group of militia marched right into the brown water, holding their rifles high above their heads. When our truck got on the bridge directly over the water, one of the Cuban newspapermen leaped out of the truck down 10 feet into the water. People in the trucks would jump right over the side, sometimes pausing to take off their shoes. Most went in shoes and all.

Now we began to wind up the narrow mountain road for the first time. All our progress since Yara had been upgrade, but this was the first time it was clearly discernible that we were going up a mountain. It took another hour to reach the top. It was afternoon now and already long lines of people were headed back down the mountain. But it was a narrow line compared to the thousands of people who were scrambling up just behind us. From one point where we stopped just before reaching the top it was possible to look down the side of the long hill and see swarms of people all the way down past the river seeming now to inch along in effortless pantomime.

The trucks stopped among a jumble of rocks and sand not quite at the top of the last grade. (For the last 20 minutes of our climb we actually had to wind in and out among groups of people. The only people who seemed to race along without any thought of the traffic were the *campesinos* on their broken-down mounts.) Now everyone began jumping down off the trucks and trying to re-form into their respective groups. It seemed almost impossible. Detachments of *campesino* militia (work shirts, blue jeans, straw hats and machetes) marched up behind us. *Milicianas* of about 12 and 13 separated our contingent, then herds of uniformed, trotting boys of about seven. "Hup, hup, hup, hup," one little boy was calling in vain as he ran behind the rest of his group. One of the girls called out "Hup, hup, hup, hup," keeping her group more orderly. Rebel soldiers wandered around everywhere, some with long, full beards, others with long, wavy black hair pulled under their blue berets or square-topped khaki caps, most of them young men in their 20s or teenagers. An old man with a full grey beard covering most of his face, except his sparkling blue eyes and the heavy black cigar stuck out of the side of his mouth, directed the comings and goings up and down this side of the mountain. He wore a huge red and black handled revolver and had a hunting knife sewn to his boot. Suddenly it seemed that I was lost in a sea of uniforms, and I couldn't see anyone I had come up the mountain with. I sat down on a rock until most of the uniforms passed. Then I could see Olga about

50 yards away waving her arms at her lost charges. There was a public address system booming full blast from what seemed the top of the hill. The voice (Celia Sánchez, Fidel's secretary) was announcing various groups that were passing in review. When we got to the top of the rise, we could see a large, austere platform covered with all kinds of people, and at the front of the platform a raised section with a dais where the speakers were Sra. Sánchez was announcing one corps of militia and they marched out of the crowd and stopped before the platform. The crowd cheered and cheered. The militia was commended from the platform and then they marched off into the crowd at the other side. Other groups marched past. Young women, teenage girls, elderly campesinos, each with their own militia detachment, each to be commended. This had been going on since morning. Hundreds of commendations, thousands of people to be commended. Also, since morning, the officials had been reading off lists of names of campesinos who were to receive land under the Agrarian Reform Law. When they read the name of some farmer close enough to the mountain to hear it, he would leap straight up in the air and, no matter how far away from the platform he was, would go barreling and leaping towards the speaker. The crowd delighted in this and would begin chanting "Viva Fidel, Viva Fidel, Viva Reforma Agraria!" All this had been going on since morning and it was now late afternoon.

After we walked past the dais, introduced to the screaming crowd as "intellectual North American visitors" we doubled back and went up onto the platform itself. It was even hotter up there. By now all I could think about was the sun; it was burning straight down and had been since early morning. I tugged the straw hat down over my eyes and trudged up onto the platform. The platform itself in back of the dais was almost overflowing, mostly with rebel soldiers and young militia troops. But there were all kinds of visitors also, the Latin American delegates, newsmen, European writers, American intellectuals, as well as Cuban officials. When we got up on the platform, Olga led us immediately over to the speakers' dais and the little group of seats around it. We were going to be introduced to all the major speakers.

The first person to turn around and greet us was a tall, thin, bearded Negro in a rebel uniform bearing the shoulder markings of a Comandante. I recognized his face from the papers as that of Juan

Almeida, chief of the rebel army, a man almost unknown in the United States. He grinned and shook our hands and talked in a swift combination of Spanish and English, joking constantly about conditions in the United States. In the middle of one of his jokes he leaned backwards, leaning over one man to tap another taller man on the shoulder. Fidel Castro leaned back in his seat, then got up smiling and came over to where we were standing. He began shaking hands with everybody in the group, as well as the many other visitors who moved in at the opportunity. There were so many people on the platform in what seemed like complete disorder that I wondered how wise it was as far as security was concerned. It seemed awfully dangerous for the Prime Minister to be walking around so casually, almost having to thread his way through the surging crowd. Almost immediately, I shoved my hand toward his face and then grasped his hand. He greeted me warmly, asking through the interpreter where I was from and what I did. When I told him I was a New York poet, he seemed extremely amused and asked me what the government thought about my trip. I shrugged my shoulders and asked him what did he intend to do with this revolution.

We both laughed at the question because it was almost like a reflex action on my part; something that came out so quick that I was almost unaware of it. He twisted the cigar in his mouth and grinned, smoothing the strangely grown beard on his cheeks. "That *is* a poet's question," he said, "and the only poet's answer I can give you is that I will do what I think is right, what I think the people want. That's the best I can hope for, don't you think?"

I nodded, already getting ready to shoot out another question, I didn't know how long I'd have. Certainly this was the most animated I'd been during the entire trip. "Uh," I tried to smile, "What do you think the United States will do about Cuba ultimately?" The questions seemed weird and out of place because everyone else was just trying to shake his hand.

"Ha, well, that's extremely difficult to say, your government is getting famous for its improvisation in foreign affairs. I suppose it depends on who is running the government. If the Democrats win it may get better. More Republicans... I suppose more trouble. I cannot say, except that I really do not care what they do as long as they do not try to interfere with the running of this country."

Suddenly the idea of a security lapse didn't seem so pressing. I had turned my head at a weird angle and looked up at the top of the platform. There was a soldier at each side of the back wall of the platform, about 10 feet off the ground, each one with a machine gun on a tripod. I asked another question. "What about communism? How big a part does that play in the government?"

"I've said a hundred times that I'm not a communist. But I am certainly not an anti-communist. The United States likes anti-communists, especially so close to their mainland. I said also a hundred times that I consider myself a humanist. A radical humanist. The only way that anything can ever be accomplished in a country like Cuba is radically. The old has been here so long that the new must make radical changes in order to function at all."

So many people had crowded around us now that it became almost impossible to hear what Fidel was saying. I had shouted the last question. A young fashion model who had come with our group brushed by me and said how much she had enjoyed her stay in Cuba. Fidel touched his hand to the wide *campesino* hat she was wearing, then pumped her hand up and down. One of the Latin American girls leaned forward suddenly and kissed him on the cheek. Everyone milled around the tall, young Cuban, asking questions, shaking his hand, taking pictures, getting autographs (an American girl with pigtails and blue jeans) and, I suppose, committing everything he said to memory. The crowd was getting too large, I touched his arm, waved, and walked towards the back of the platform.

I hadn't had any water since early morning, and the heat and the excitement made my mouth dry and hard. There were no water fountains in sight. Most of the masses of Cubans had canteens or vacuum bottles, but someone had forgotten to tell the Americans (North and South) that there would be no water. Also, there was no shade at all on the platform. I walked around behind it and squatted in a small booth with a tiny tin roof. It had formerly been a soda stand, but because the soda was free, the supply had given out rapidly and the stand had closed. I sat in the few inches of shade with my head in my hands, trying to cool off. Some Venezuelans came by and asked to sit in the shade next to me. I said it was all right and they offered me the first cup of water I'd had in about five hours. They had a whole chicken also, but I didn't think I'd be able to stand the luxury.

There were more speakers, including a little boy from one of the youngest militia units, but I heard them all over the public address system. I was too beat and thirsty to move. Later Ed Clarke and I went around hunting for water and finally managed to find a small brown stream where the soldiers were filling up their canteens. I drank two coca-cola bottles full, and when I got back to Havana came down with a fearful case of dysentery.

Suddenly there was an insane deafening roar from the crowd. I met the girl economist as I dragged myself out of the booth and she tried to get me to go back on the front platform. Fidel was about to speak. I left her and jumped off the platform and trotted up a small rise to the left. The roar lasted about 10 minutes, and as I got settled on the side of the hill Fidel began to speak.

He is an amazing speaker, knowing probably instinctively all the laws of dynamics and elocution. The speech began slowly and haltingly, each syllable being pronounced with equal stress, as if he were reading a poem. He was standing with the *campesino* hat pushed back slightly off his forehead, both hands on the lectern. As he made his points, one of the hands would slide off the lectern and drop to his side, his voice becoming tighter and less warm. When the speech was really on its way, he dropped both hands from the lectern, putting one behind his back like a church usher, gesturing with the other. By now he would be rocking from side to side, pointing his finger at the crowd, at the sky, at his own chest. Sometimes he seemed to lean to the side and talk to his own ministers there on that platform with him and then wheel towards the crowd calling for them to support him. At one point in the speech the crowd interrupted for about 20 minutes crying "Venceremos, venceremos, venceremos, venceremos, venceremos, venceremos, venceremos, venceremos." The entire crowd, 60 or 70,000 people all chanting in unison. Fidel stepped away from the lectern grinning, talking to his aides. He quieted the crowd with a wave of his arms and began again. At first softly, with the syllables drawn out and precisely enunciated, then tightening his voice and going into an almost musical rearrangement of his speech. He condemned Eisenhower, Nixon, the South, the Monroe Doctrine, the Platt Amendment, and Fulgencio Batista in one long unbelievable sentence. The crowd interrupted again, "Fidel, Fidel, Fidel, Fidel, Fidel, Fidel, Fidel, Fidel, Fidel, Fidel, Fidel." He leaned away from the lectern grinning at the chief of the army. The speech lasted almost two-and-a-half hours, being interrupted time and again by the exultant crowd and once by five minutes of rain. Almeida draped a rain jacket around Fidel's shoulders, and he re-lit his cigar. When the speech ended, the crowd went out of its head, roaring for almost 45 minutes.

When the speech was over, I made a fast move for the platform. Almost a thousand other people had the same idea. I managed to shout something to Castro as he was being whizzed to the back of the platform and into a car. I shouted, "A fine speech, a tremendous speech."

He shouted back, "I hope you take it home with you," and disappeared in a host of bearded uniforms.

We were told at first that we would be able to leave the mountain in about three hours. But it had gotten dark already, and I didn't really fancy shooting down that mountain road with the same exuberance with which we came... not in the dark, Clarke and I went out looking for more water and walked almost a mile before we came to a big pavilion where soft drinks and sandwiches were being served. The soft drinks were hot and the sandwiches took too long to get. We came back and lay down at the top of a hill in back of the speakers' platform. It drizzled a little bit and the ground was patently uncomfortable. I tried to go to sleep but was awakened in a few minutes by explosions. The whole sky was lit up. Green, red, bright orange: the soldiers were shooting off fireworks. The platform was bathed in the light from the explosions and, suddenly, floodlights from the rear. The public address system announced that we were going to have a show.

The show was a strange mixture of pop culture and mainstream highbrow "haute culture." There was a choral group singing a mildly atonal tone poem, a Jerome Robbinsesque ballet about Hollywood, Calypso dancers, and Mexican singers and dancers. The last act was the best, a Mardi Gras scene involving about a hundred West Indian singers and dancers, complete with floats, huge papier-mache figures, drummers, and masks. The West Indians walked through the audience shouting and dancing, their many torches shooting shadows against the mountains. When they danced off and out of the amphitheatre area up towards a group of unfinished school buildings, except for the huge floodlights on stage, the whole area was dark. Now there was great confusion in the audience. Most Cubans were still going to try to get home that night, so they were getting themselves together, rounding up wives and children, trying to find some kind of transportation off the mountain. There were still whole units of militia piling into trucks or walking off down the hill in the dark. The delegates, our group and a couple more thousand people who didn't feel like charging off into the dark were left. Olga got all the Americans together, and we lined up for what was really our first meal of the day: beans, rice, pork, and a small can of fruit juice. At that time, we still had some hopes of leaving that night, but soon word was passed around that we weren't leaving, and it was best that we slept where we were. "Sleep wherever you want," was what Olga said. That meant the ground, or maybe cement sidewalks around the unfinished school buildings and dormitories of the new "school city." Some of the Americans started grumbling, but there was nothing that could be done. Two of our number were missing because of the day's festivities: a young lady from Philadelphia had to be driven back to Havana in a station wagon because she had come down with diarrhea and a fever; and the model who had walked around without her hat too often and had gotten a slight case of sunstroke. She was resting up in the medical shack now, and I began to envy her small canvas cot.

It was a very strange scene, about 3,000 to 4,000 people wandering around in semi-darkness among a group of unfinished buildings, looking for places to sleep. The whole top of the mountain alive with flashlights, cigarette lighters, and small torches. Little groups of people huddled together against the sides of buildings or stretched out under new "street lamps" in temporary plazas. Some people managed to climb through the windows of the new buildings and sleep on dirt floors, some slept under long aluminum trucks used for hauling stage equipment and some, like myself and the young female economist, sat up all night under dim lights, finally talking ourselves excitedly to sleep in the cool gray of early morning. I lay straight back on the cement "sidewalk" and slept without moving, until the sun began to burn my face.

We had been told the night before to be ready by six a.m. to pull out, but when morning came we loitered around again till about eight o'clock, when we had to line up for a breakfast of hot milk and French bread. It was served by young militia women, one of whom wore a big sidearm in a shoulder holster. By now, the dysentery was beginning to play havoc with my stomach, and the only toilet was a heavy thicket out behind the amphitheatre. I made it once, having to destroy a copy of a newspaper with my picture in it.

By nine no trucks had arrived, and with the sun now beginning to move heavily over us, the crowds shifted into the few shady areas remaining. It looked almost as if there were as many people still up on the mountain as there had been when we first arrived. Most of the Cubans, aside from the soldiers, stood in front of the pavilion and drank luke-warm Maltina or pineapple soda. The delegates and the other visitors squatted against buildings, talking and smoking. A French correspondent made a bad joke about Mussolini keeping the trains running on time, and a young Chinese student asked him why he wasn't in Algeria killing rebels.

The trucks did arrive, but there were only enough of them to take the women out. In a few minutes the sides of the trucks were almost bursting, so many females had stuffed inside. And they looked terribly uncomfortable, especially the ones stuck in the center who couldn't move an inch either way. An American newspaperman with our group who was just about to overstay his company-sanctioned leave began to panic, saying that the trucks wouldn't be back until the next day. But only a half-hour after the ladies pulled out, more trucks came and began taking the men out. Clarke, Williams, another member of our group and I sat under the tin roof of an unfinished school building drinking warm soda, waiting until the last truck came, hoping it would be the least crowded. When we did climb up into one of the trucks it was jammed anyway, but we felt it was time to move.

This time we all had to stand up, except for a young *miliciano* who was squatting on a case of warm soda. I was in the center of the crowd and had nothing to hold on to but my companions. Every time the truck would stop short, which it did every few yards we traveled, everyone in the truck was slung against everyone else. When the truck did move, however, it literally zoomed down the side of the mountain. But then we would stop again, and all of us felt we would suffocate being mashed so tightly together, and from all the dust the trucks in front of us kicked up. The road now seemed like the Exodus. Exactly the same as the day before, only headed the opposite way. The trucks, the people on foot, the families, the militias, the *campesinos*, all headed down the mountain.

The truck sat one place 20 minutes without moving, and then when it did move it only edged up a few yards. Finally the driver pulled out of the main body of traffic and honking his horn continuously drove down the opposite side of the road. When the soldiers directing traffic managed to flag him down, he told them that we were important visitors who had to make a train in Yara. The truck zoomed off again, rocking back and forth and up and down, throwing its riders at times almost out the back gate.

After a couple of miles, about five Mexicans got off the truck and got into another truck headed for Santiago. This made the rest of the ride easier. The *miliciano* began opening the semi-chilled soda and passing it around. We were really living it up. The delegates' spirits came back and they started their chanting and waving. When we got to the train junction, the cattle cars were sitting, but completely filled with soldiers and farmers. We didn't even stop, the driver gunned the thing as fast as it would go and we sailed by the shouting soldiers. We had only a few more stops before we got to Yara, jumped down in the soft sand, and ran for the big silver train marked "CUBA" that had been waiting for us since we left. When we got inside the train we discovered that the women still hadn't gotten back, so we sat quietly in the luxurious leather seats slowly sipping rum. The women arrived an hour later.

While we were waiting in Yara, soldiers and units of militia began to arrive in the small town and squat all around the four or five sets of tracks waiting for their own trains. Most of them went back in boxcars, while we visitors had the luxury of the semi-air-conditioned coach.

The ride back was even longer than the 14 hours it took us before. Once when we stopped for water, we sat about two hours. Later, we stopped to pick up lunches. The atmosphere in the train was much the same as before, especially the Mexican delegates who whooped it up constantly. They even made a conga line up and down the whole length of the train. The young Mexican woman and I did a repeat performance also and talked most of the 15 or 16 hours it took us to get back to Havana. She was gentler with me this time, calling me "Yanqui imperialist" only a few times.

Everyone in the train was dirty, thirsty, and tired when we arrived in Havana. I had been wearing the same clothes for three days and hadn't even once taken off my shoes. The women were in misery. I hadn't seen a pocket mirror since the cattle cars.

The terminal looked like a rear outpost of some battlefield. So many people in filthy wrinkled clothes scrambling wearily out of trains. But even as tired as I was I felt excited at the prospect of being back in the big city for 5 more days, I was even more excited by the amount of thinking the trip to the Sierra was forcing me to. The "new" ideas that were being shoved at me, some of which I knew would be painful when I eventually came to New York.

The idea of "a revolution" had been foreign to me. It was one of those inconceivably "romantic" and/or hopeless ideas that we *Norteamericanos* have been taught since public school to hold up to the cold light of "reason." That "reason" being whatever repugnant lie our usurious "ruling class" had paid their journalists to disseminate. The "reason" that allows that voting, in a country where the parties are exactly the same, can be made to assume the gravity of actual moral engagement. The "reason" that permits a young intellectual to believe he has said something profound when he says, "I don't trust men in uniforms." The *residue* has settled on all our lives, and no one can function comfortably in this country without it. That thin crust of lie we cannot even detect in our own thinking. That rotting of the mind which had enabled us to think about Hiroshima as if someone else had done it, or to believe vaguely that the "counter-revolution" in Guatemala was an "internal" affair.

The rebels among us have become merely people like myself who grow beards and will not participate in politics. A bland revolt. Drugs, juvenile delinquency, complete isolation from the vapid more of the country — a few current ways out. But name an alternative here. Something not inextricably bound up in a lie. Something not part of liberal stupidity or the actual filth of vested interest. There is none. It's much too late. We are an *old* people already. Even the vitality of our art is like bright flowers growing up through a rotting carcass.

But the Cubans, and the other *new* peoples (in Asia, Africa, South America) don't need us, and we had better stay out of their way.

I came out of the terminal into the street and stopped at a newsstand to buy a newspaper. The headlines of one Miami paper read, "CUBAN CELEBRATION RAINED OUT." I walked away from the stand as fast as I could.

Reprinted with permission of the author

Cuba —
A declaration of conscience by Afro-Americans

The Afro-American
April 22, 1961

Because we have known oppression, because we have suffered more than other Americans, because we are still fighting for our own liberation from tyranny, we Afro-Americans have the right and the duty to raise our voices in protest against the forces of oppression that now seek to crush a free people linked to us by bonds of blood and a common heritage.

One-third of Cuba's people are Afro-Cubans, of the same African descent as we. Many of our own forefathers passed through Cuba on their way to the slave plantations in the United States. Those who remained on the island knew the same brutality that their brothers suffered on the mainland; after emancipation, they too knew disenfranchisement, they too became second-class citizens, peons exploited on the huge U.S.-owned landholdings. Today — thanks to a social revolution which they helped make — Afro-Cubans are first-class citizens and are taking their rightful place in the life of their country where all racial barriers crumbled in a matter of weeks following the victory of Fidel Castro. As Joseph Newman reported in the *New York Herald-Tribune* (March 23): "Castro and Guevara are literally adored by the large number of poor and humiliated Cubans, especially the Negroes. They see these two leaders as saintly and honorable men, dedicated to removing injustices and discrimination."

Now our brothers are threatened again — this time by a gang of ousted white Cuban politicians who find segregated Miami more congenial than integrated Havana. We charge that this group of mercenaries who hope to turn back the clock in Cuba are armed, trained and financed by the U.S. Central Intelligence Agency. But they know that by themselves that can never re-enslave the Cuban people, so now they are openly boasting that U.S. troops will go to their aid as soon as they land in Cuba. This criminal aggression against a peaceful and progressive people must not be allowed to happen. But if it does, we are determined to do all we possibly can to hinder the success of this crime.

Afro-American correspondent William Worthy declared recently: "If Cuba is attacked, I and others who know the facts will denounce the attack as an evil and wicked colonial war deserving of opposition and resistance by Afro-Americans." Worthy warned that, if such an attack took place: "In this country we would see civil rights setbacks from coast to coast. Our enemies would be strengthened and emboldened."

Afro-Americans, don't be fooled – the enemies of the Cubans are our enemies, the Jim Crow bosses of this land where we are still denied our rights. The Cubans are our friends, the enemies our enemies.

Emmett Basset	Walter Bowe	Edward Clark
John Henrik Clarke	Odessa Cox	Dr. Lonnie Cross
Harold Cruse	Felix A. Cummings	Dr. W. E. B. DuBois
Shirley Graham	Calvin Hicks	LeRoi Jones
Jane Kerina	Conrad Lynn	Julian Mayfield
Robert C. Maynard	John W. McDow	Marion Metelits
Carlos Moore	Nanny Murrell	Clarence H. Seniors
John A. Singleton	Pernella Wattley	Daniel H. Watts
Robert F. Williams	William Worth	

Richard Gibson
Acting Executive Secretary, Fair Play for Cuba Committee

Declaration of the African American delegation

Malcolm X Speaks in the 90s Symposium

Havana, Cuba
May 19-25, 1990

We the undersigned members of the African American delegation to the *Malcolm X Speaks in the 90s Symposium* held in Havana, Cuba (May 18-25, 1990) make the following declaration:

In the United States at this time, popular forms of resistance are emerging to defend Black people against genocidal social conditions and violent racist attacks. Malcolm X is a central political symbol of this resistance. This is a major opportunity to deepen our understanding of the radical Black tradition, to 'open broad based community discussion and debate critical ideological and political issues, and to forge greater unity in our liberation struggle through alliances, coalitions, fronts and joint statements of unity.

We recognize, acknowledge and deeply appreciate the tremendous sacrifices that the Cuban people and its government have paid in human lives and material resources in advancing the cause of Black liberation, both on the African continent and in the African diaspora, including the granting of asylum and sanctuary to political prisoners opposing U.S. racism and imperialism.

Therefore, in this spirit we declare the following:

a. We call upon all African peoples and progressive forces to rededicate themselves to the struggle for Black liberation, including political, economic and social justice, as well as the fight for human rights in the tradition of Malcolm X.

b. We deplore and oppose with all our moral and political convictions the insidious U.S. effort to intervene in the internal affairs of Cuba, attack the Cuban people and turn back the gains of their revolution. We unequivocally condemn the U.S. government's systematic attacks: the continued economic blockade, menacing the people of Cuba with the threat of military invasion, illegal media propaganda campaigns to sow seeds of reaction inside Cuba, particularly the lies, disinformation and slander the U.S. promotes as "news." We understand that this is intended to creative a grave crisis to undermine the national sovereignty and territorial integrity of Cuba, and thus we demand:

1) that the U.S. government cease and desist from all its efforts to intimidate Cuba and its people, lift its immoral economic blockade, and call upon all progressive countries and organizations in the world to join us in this demand;

2) that in the spirit of both Malcolm X and José Martí, to strengthen our solidarity with Cuba, we call upon all African peoples and progressive organizations to join in an international information exchange program whereby we will provide Cuba with information from INSIDE THE MONSTER while Cuba will send the people in the USA information from INSIDE THE REVOLUTION as an effort to combat the illegal radio and television aggression, especially so-called Radio and TV Martí.

3) We call upon all African peoples and progressive forces to join in building an active mass campaign of information and direct action protests to mobilize the American people around the important and urgent issue of keeping *U.S. Hands Off Cuba*.

4) We call upon all African peoples and progressive forces to involve themselves in efforts to expose the violation of human rights inside the United States. We remind the world of the scores of political prisoners currently being held in U.S. prisons and detention centers. We support the Universal Declaration of Human Rights as socially just principles which are not respected by the United States in terms of its

relationship with African Americans and other oppressed nationalities.

5) We call upon all African peoples and progressive forces to support the movement to Save the Audubon Ballroom, the site where Malcolm X was assassinated, and denounce the plan by Columbia University and New York City to destroy this historic landmark and build in its place biomedical technology experimental laboratories. We call instead for the Audubon Ballroom to be renovated and developed into an international cultural center in Malcolm's name where our youth can study his life, his rise from the depths of U.S. society to a world renowned international statesman for human rights. The Malcolm X Cultural Center would also serve as an institution to study Malcolm's predecessors, contemporaries and progenies who struggled for the right to self-determination and national identity of Africans in the United States and the Americas.

6) We call upon all African peoples and progressive forces to establish the birthday of Malcolm X as an African people's national holiday, to commemorate his contributions and their relations to other international heroes whose lives also are commemorated on or about the 19th of May.

7) We call upon all African peoples and progressive forces to actively build and participate in the *International Conference on Malcolm X: Radical Tradition and a Legacy of Struggle* to be held November 1-4, 1990 in New York City.

We are forever grateful to Casa de las Américas and the Center for the Study of the Americas for answering our call to host this symposium. We have gained immensely from our Cuban brothers and sisters and were pleased to share with them the experiences of our brother and great son Malcolm X — a dedicated fighter for self-determination and human rights of oppressed peoples throughout the world. But even more than this we are grateful for the Cuban example that Revolution is possible, that there is a glorious possibility that the centuries old degradation of capitalist exploitation can — and will — be surpassed.

For this we salute Cuba in this declaration and commit ourselves to deepen our solidarity with the Cuban Revolution as we advance our common struggle for peace and social justice through the programs we hereby adopt by the signing of this document.

Done this day, the 25th of May, 1990 by the African American Delegation to the *Malcolm X Speaks in the 90s Symposium*, May 18-25 in Havana, Cuba.

Akiwumi, Viki
Alkalimat, Abdul
Brath, Elombe
Clay, Omowale
Hernandez, Lewanda
Lawrence Lucas, Father
Mealy, Rosemari
Monteiro, Tony
Muhammad, Ahmad
Polintan-Taverna, Odette

Rabab, Sulaiman
Russell, Natasha
Sales, William
Samad-Matias, Marguerita
Shakur, Assata
Strickland, William
Toure, Kwame
Turner, James
Umoja, Akinyele

Notes on contributors

Bill Epton's first political experience was as a child watching a parade of Garveyites along Harlem's Lenox Avenue in 1937. He will never forget the exhilarating of seeing those Black men on horseback proudly marching down the avenue. In high school, Epton was active in the Young Communist League where he sold the *Daily Worker* newspaper, passed out leaflets and supported various strikes.

In 1960, Epton left the Communist Party USA and went on to help form the Progressive Labor Party, which he was with for a number of years. Bill has been active in the Black liberation movement and currently runs a print shop in Harlem, where he lives with his wife Beryl.

Sarah E. Wright has published a number of poems, book reviews and articles in various journals. Her epic poem, "To Some Millions who Survive" was re-published in Cuba's *Revolucion*, during her visit to the island in 1960. Her first novel, *This Child's Gonna Live*, an African-North American saga was hailed as a "masterpiece" by the *New York Times Book Review*.

Wright's latest book, *A. Philip Randolph, Integration in the Workplace* was awarded the "Best Book" prize for young adults by the New York Public Libraries in 1991. She was elected President of Pen and Brush, Inc. in 1992.

Elombe Brath for more than a decade has committed his life to the study of African culture while organizing and speaking out against the injustices of the African American community throughout the United States. A prolific writer and historian, in the late 1950s he was a founding member of the African Jazz-Art Society and Studies (AJASS), a vanguard organization which spearheaded the concept of Black is Beauty in the United States, resulting in changing the philosophical outlook of the entire African American community. He was also a writer and political cartoonist for the *New York Citizen-Call*. Brath was a founding member of the Patrice Lumumba Coalition along with the late Irving Davis, which threw its full support behind the national liberation and independence movements in Angola and Namibia, represented by the MPLA and SWAPO. He lives in Harlem with his wife Nomsa and family.

Amiri Baraka (LeRoi Jones) is a political activist and the author of over 20 plays, two jazz operas, seven books of nonfiction, and over a dozen volumes of poetry. He has received grants from the Rockefeller Foundation and the National Endowment for the Arts, has taught at Columbia, Yale, the State University of New York at Stony Brook and New Jersey's Rutgers University. In 1960, as poet and editor of *Yugen* magazine, he was among a group of African Americans invited to Cuba on a trip arranged by the Fair Play for Cuba Committee. He and his wife Amina, also a noted poet, live in Newark, New Jersey.

Rosemari Mealy is a poet, essayist, radio producer and freelance journalist who lived in Cuba in 1985-87. She has written for both national and international news agencies and her work has appeared in numerous literary journals and anthologies. She is the author of *Lift these shadows from our eyes* [West End Press]. Currently she serves on the executive committee of the National Venceremos Brigade and is an NGO representative for the National Alliance of Third World Journalists at the United Nations. She resides in New York City with her husband Sam Anderson.

Index

African Nationalist Movement, 46

African Nationalist Pioneer Movement, 29

Afro-American, 79-80

Akiwumi, Viki, 84

Ali, Muhammad, 48, 51, 56

Alkalimat, Abdul, 84

Almeida Bosque, Juan, 18, 52, 53, 61, 70-71

Amsterdam News, 41, 47, 54

Azekewi, Nnamdi, 15

Bandung Conference, 28

Baraka, Amiri (LeRoi Jones), 62-78, 80, 85

Batista, Fulgencio, 4, 10, 23, 25, 45, 49, 73

Beals, Carleton, 51

Bisbé Alberni, Manuel Dr., 32

Black Muslim movement, 58

Booker, Jimmy, 41, 45, 46-48

Bowe, Walter, 80

Brath, Elombe, 27-31, 84, 85

Cartier-Bresson, Henri, 50

Casa de las Américas (Casa), 2, 6, 7

Chicago Defender, 57

CIA, 11, 37, 44

CIO (Congress of Industrial Organizations), 15

Clark, Edward, 67, 73, 76, 80

Clarke, John Henrik, 21, 80

Clay, Omowale, 84

Communist Party of the USA, 12, 14, 15, 19, 85

Congress of Racial Equality, 29

Cooks, Carlos, A., 29, 30

Cox, Odessa, 80

Cross, Lonnie, Dr., 80

Cruse, Harold, 80

Cummings, Felix A., 80

Current, Gloster B., 54

Davis, Ben, 12, 19

Davis, Clarence, 7

Dixon, Jim, 35

DuBois, W. E. B. Dr., 80

DuPonts, 64

Ebony magazine, 57

Eisenhower, Dwight D., 32, 55, 64, 73

Epton, William (Bill), 14-20, 54, 85

Essien-Udom, D.E.U., 29, 30

Fair Play for Cuba Committee, 12, 35, 49-50, 62

Farmer, James, 29

FBI, 37, 44

Garvey movement, 29

Garvey, Marcus, Honorable, 14, 30

Gibson, Richard, 50, 80

Ginsberg, Allen, 50

87

Graham, Shirley, 80
Gray, Jesse, 17
Guevara, Che, 10, 13, 58-59, 63
Guy, Rosa, 21

Hammarskjold, Dag, 35, 37, 38,
    40
Harlem Writers Guild, 21
Hernandez, Lewanda, 84
Hicks, Calvin, 80
Hughes, Langston, 50

Johnson, Booker, 29, 36, 51-52,
    53, 55, 56
July 26 Movement, 4, 10, 49, 62

Kerina, Jane, 80
Khrushchev, Nikita, 12, 13, 20,
    22, 37
Killens, John Oliver, 21
King, Martin Luther, Dr., 28, 29
KKK, 15, 16, 59

Lawrence Lucas, Father, 84
Lawson, James Rupert, 29, 46
Lincoln, Abraham, 43, 50
Lost-Found Nation of Islam, 28
Louis, Joe, 51
Louis X, 52
Lower Harlem Tenants
    Council, 17
Lumumba, Patrice, 43
Lynn, Conrad, 9, 35-37, 52-53, 80

Malcolm X Speaks in the 90's
    Symposium, 2-9, 59-61,
    81-84
Mandela, Nelson, 14, 18
Martí, José, 51, 82
Matthews, Ralph D., 41-44
Mayfield, Julian, 80
Maynard, Robert C., 80
McCarthy period, 15, 16
McDow, John W., 80

Mealy, Rosemari, 84, 85
Metelits, Marion, 80
Moncada Barracks, 4, 10, 49
Monteiro, Tony, 84
Moore, Carlos, 17, 80
Muhammad Speaks, 18, 57
Muhammad, Ahmad, 44, 84
Muhammad, Elijah, The
    Honorable, 27-28
Muhammad, Everett, 57
Muhammad, Walie, 56
Murrell, Nanny, 80

NAACP, 54
Nasser, Gamal Abdel, 12, 20, 37
Nation of Islam (NOI), 19, 27,
    29, 31, 51, 56
Negro American Labor
    Council (NALC), 17
Nehru, Jawaharlal, 13, 20
Nesfield, Carl, 41, 44, 46
New York Citizen-Call, 41, 44,
    48-49, 85
New York Daily News, 7
New York Times, 34, 54
Nixon, Richard, 32, 64, 73
Nkrumah, Kwame, 13, 15
Noble Drew, Ali, 28

Operation Truth, 57

Parks, Rosa, 16
Peñalver, Reinaldo, 8, 48, 50-51,
    53-55, 57-58
Polintan-Taverna, Odette, 84
Powell, Adam Clayton Jr., 54

Rabab, Sulaiman, 84
Randolph, A. Philip, 16
Roa Kouri, Raúl, 8 32-35, 56
Rosa Blanca (The White Rose),
    33, 48, 54
Russell, Natasha, 84

Sales, William (Bill), 84
Samad-Matias, Margarita, 84
Sánchez, Celia, 70
Sartre, Jean Paul, 40
Seniors, Clarence, 80
Shakur, Assata, 3, 5, 84
Shelley, Jaime, 64
Sierra Maestra, 10, 57, 62
Silver, Dave, 37
Singleton, John A., 80
Stokley Carmichael (see
    Kwame Toure)
Strickland, William, 84
Supreme Wisdom, 29

Taber, Robert (Bob), 32, 35, 49
Till, Emmett, 16
Toure, Kwame, (Stokley
    Carmichael), 3, 84
Turner, James, 84

U.S. State Department, 21, 26,
    40, 58
Umoja, Akinyele, 84
United African National
    Movement, 29

Venceremos Brigade, 85

Wallace, Mike, 30
Wattley, Pernella, 80
Watts, Daniel H., 80
Wilcox, Preston, 37
Wilkins, Roy, 29
Williams, Robert F., 53, 66, 76,
    80
Wood, Love B., 8, 35-36, 51, 54,
    55
Worthy, William, 80
Wright, Sarah Elizabeth, 20-22,
    85

Young, Whitney, 29